D1358431

DIABETIC LIVING Everyday COOKING

VOLUME 10

DIABETIC LIVING® EVERYDAY COOKING
IS PART OF A BOOK SERIES PUBLISHED BY
BETTER HOMES AND GARDENS SPECIAL
INTEREST MEDIA, DES MOINES, IOWA

Chicken, Tomato, and Cucumber Salad
recipe, *p. 37*

Start with nutritionally balanced recipes for meal plan success.

A diagnosis of prediabetes or diabetes can seem overwhelming and scary. But once you discover what you should and shouldn't eat and implement an exercise plan for a healthy lifestyle, you are well on your way to taking control and feeling better.

When you're looking for good-for-you recipes, grab this edition of *Everyday Cooking*. It's filled with delicious dishes that are perfect for ensuring your meals are nutritionally balanced. And the whole family will love them, too!

This book is a great kitchen companion—all of the recipes have been tested and tasted by a team of kitchen professionals and editors to make sure they are accurate, easy to prepare, and tasty. The *Diabetic Living*® dietitians have fine-tuned the ingredients to ensure that each recipe offers a healthful tally of calories, fat, carbohydrate, and sodium. Look for the easy-to-read nutritional profile at the end of every recipe.

Thumb through these pages to discover tasty, family-style breakfast, lunch, and dinner ideas that will please everyone. And remember, snacking is important, too. You'll find satisfying recipes for nibbles that will help to keep your blood sugars in check between meals.

This volume is one of the best yet! Head to the kitchen to discover great tastes and new favorites!

ON THE COVER:
Grilled Asparagus and Shrimp with Pasta
recipe, *p. 28*

Photographer: Blaine Moats
Food Stylist: Dianna Nolin

82

109

152

EDITORIAL ADVISORY BOARD

The following experts review articles that appear in *Diabetic Living®* magazine:

Sheri R. Colberg, Ph.D., FACSM, professor emerita of exercise science at Old Dominion University; 2016 ADA Outstanding Diabetes Educator

Marjorie Cypress, Ph.D., CNP, CDE, Albuquerque-based consultant; past president of health care and education, ADA

Joanne Gallivan, M.S., RDN, National Diabetes Education Program director at the NIH

Sharonne N. Hayes, M.D., FACC, FAHA, cardiologist and founder of the Women's Heart Clinic at Mayo Clinic

Manny Hernandez, Diabetes Hands Foundation cofounder; executive at Livongo Health

Marty Irons, RPh, CDE, community pharmacist, author; served in industry and military

Francine R. Kaufman, M.D., chief medical officer and vice president of Global Medical Affairs at Medtronic Diabetes

Nathan A. Painter, Pharm.D., CDE, associate clinical professor at UC San Diego Skaggs School of Pharmacy

Chef Art Smith, Florida-based star of Bravo's *Top Chef Masters* and former personal chef for Oprah Winfrey

Hope S. Warshaw, M.M.Sc., RD, CDE, author of *Diabetes Meal Planning Made Easy* and *Eat Out, Eat Well,* published by the ADA

John Zrebiec, M.S.W., CDE, director of Behavioral Health Services at the Joslin Diabetes Center and lecturer in psychiatry at Harvard Medical School

---

GUIDE TO CREDENTIALS:
CDE: Diabetes educator, **CNP:** Nurse practitioner, **FACC:** American College of Cardiology fellow, **FACSM:** American College of Sports Medicine fellow, **FAHA:** American Heart Association fellow, **M.D.:** Doctor of Medicine, **M.M.Sc.:** Master of Medical Science, **M.S.:** Master of Science, **M.S.W.:** Master of Social Work, **RD:** Dietitian, **RDN:** Dietitian nutritionist, **Pharm.D.:** Doctor of Pharmacy, **Ph.D.:** Doctor of Philosophy, **RPh:** pharmacist

CONSUMER MARKETING

Vice President, Consumer Marketing	STEVE CROWE
Consumer Marketing Product Director	HEATHER SORENSEN
Consumer Marketing Billing/Renewal Manager	TAMI PERKINS
Consumer Marketing Product Manager	WENDY MERICAL
Business Director	DIANE UMLAND
Production Manager	AL RODRUCK
Contributing Project Manager	SHELLI MCCONNELL, PURPLE PEAR PUBLISHING, INC.
Contributing Photographer	JASON WALSMITH
Contributing Food Stylist	DIANNA NOLIN
Test Kitchen Director	LYNN BLANCHARD
Test Kitchen Chef	CARLA CHRISTIAN, RD, LD

DIABETIC LIVING® MAGAZINE

Editorial DIrector	JENNIFER DARLING
Executive Editor	JENNIFER WILSON
Creative Director	MICHAEL BELKNAP
Senior Associate Editor	CAITLYN DIIMIG, RD
Associate Editor	BAILEY MCGRATH
Art Director	NIKKI SANDERS
Art Director	DEB BERGER
Administrative Assistant	LORI EGGERS

MEREDITH NATIONAL MEDIA GROUP

President JON WERTHER

Chairman and Chief Executive Officer **STEPHEN M. LACY**

Vice Chairman **MELL MEREDITH FRAZIER**

In Memoriam— **E.T. MEREDITH III (1933–2003)**

Diabetic Living® Everyday Cooking is part of a series published by Meredith Corp., 1716 Locust St., Des Moines, IA 50309-3023.

If you have comments or questions about the editorial material in *Diabetic Living® Everyday Cooking,* write to the editor of *Diabetic Living* magazine, Meredith Corp., 1716 Locust St., Des Moines, IA 50309-3023. Send an e-mail to *diabeticlivingmeredith.com* or call 800/678-2651. *Diabetic Living®* magazine is available by subscription or on the newsstand. To order a subscription to the magazine, go to *DiabeticLivingOnline.com*

© Meredith Corporation 2018. All rights reserved.

First edition. Printed in U.S.A.

ISSN 1943-2887   ISBN 978-0696-30266-4

CONTENTS

1

FAMILY-PLEASING
DINNERS

Make dinnertime a priority even during busy weekdays with

health-smart recipes you'll feel great serving. Enjoy kid-friendly

Loaded Taco Sweet Potatoes, veggie-packed Chicken Pasta

Primavera, sheet-pan Chicken Sausage and Peppers, and weekend-

special but weeknight-easy Seafood Boil.

4. Grill chicken skewers, covered, over medium-high 6 to 8 minutes or until chicken is no longer pink, turning once. Remove from grill and brush with the reserved ¼ cup marinade. Serve with Mediterranean Couscous, lemon wedges, and, if desired, fennel fronds.

Mediterranean Couscous In a small saucepan heat **1 tsp. olive oil** over medium. Add **½ cup Israeli (large pearl) couscous.** Cook and stir about 4 minutes or until light brown. Add **1 cup water.** Bring to boiling; reduce heat. Simmer, covered, about 10 minutes or until couscous is tender and liquid is absorbed, adding **½ cup snipped dried tomatoes (not oil-packed)** the last 5 minutes; cool. Transfer couscous to a large bowl. Stir in **¾ cup chopped red sweet pepper, ½ cup each chopped cucumber and chopped red onion, ⅓ cup plain fat-free Greek yogurt, ¼ cup each thinly sliced fresh basil leaves and snipped fresh parsley, 1 Tbsp. lemon juice,** and **¼ tsp. each salt and black pepper.**

PER SERVING (2 kabobs + ¾ cup couscous each) **CAL** 332, **FAT** 9 g (1 g sat. fat), **CHOL** 83 mg, **SODIUM** 360 mg, **CARB** 28 g (2 g fiber, 6 g sugars), **PRO** 32 g

Chicken Souvlaki Kabobs with Mediterranean Couscous

28 g
CARB

SERVES 4
HANDS ON 50 min.
TOTAL 2 hr. 25 min.

- 1 lb. skinless, boneless chicken breast halves, cut into ½-inch strips
- 1 cup sliced fennel (reserve fronds, if desired)
- ⅓ cup dry white wine
- ¼ cup lemon juice
- 3 Tbsp. canola oil
- 4 cloves garlic, minced
- 2 tsp. dried oregano, crushed
- ½ tsp. salt
- ¼ tsp. black pepper

- 1 recipe Mediterranean Couscous
  Lemon wedges

1. Place chicken and fennel in a resealable plastic bag set in a shallow dish. For marinade, in a bowl stir together the next seven ingredients (through pepper). Remove ¼ cup of the marinade.
2. Pour the remaining marinade over chicken mixture. Seal bag; turn to coat. Marinate in the refrigerator 1½ hours, turning bag once.
3. Meanwhile, if using wooden skewers, soak eight 10- to 12-inch skewers in water 30 minutes. Drain chicken, discarding marinade and fennel. Thread chicken, accordion-style, onto skewers.

Orange Chicken Thighs with Cauliflower Rice

9 g
CARB

SERVES 4
HANDS ON 45 min.
TOTAL 1 hr. 15 min.

- Nonstick cooking spray
- 2 Tbsp. sesame oil (not toasted)
- 4 large bone-in chicken thighs (about 2¼ lb. total), skin removed
- 1 orange
- 1 Tbsp. reduced-sodium soy sauce
- 1 Tbsp. rice vinegar
- 1 Tbsp. brown sugar
- ¼ tsp. crushed red pepper
- 2 Tbsp. cold water
- 1 tsp. cornstarch

Chicken Souvlaki Kabobs with Mediterranean Couscous

4 cups coarsely chopped cauliflower florets
½ tsp. kosher salt
⅛ tsp. black pepper
Snipped fresh cilantro (optional)

1. Preheat oven to 375°F. Coat a 2-qt. square baking dish with cooking spray. In a 12-inch nonstick skillet, heat 1 Tbsp. of the sesame oil over medium-high. Cook chicken in hot oil 10 minutes, turning to brown evenly. Arrange chicken in a single layer in prepared dish. Drain and discard drippings from skillet.

2. Remove 1 tsp. zest and squeeze 1 Tbsp. juice from orange. (If desired, set aside additional zest for garnish.) In a bowl whisk together zest, juice, and the next six ingredients (through cornstarch). Add to skillet; cook and stir until thickened and bubbly. Pour sauce over chicken in dish.

3. Bake, uncovered, about 30 minutes or until chicken is done (175°F).

4. Meanwhile, place cauliflower in a food processor. Cover and pulse until cauliflower is evenly chopped into rice-size pieces.

5. Heat the remaining 1 Tbsp. oil in the skillet over medium-high; add the cauliflower, salt, and pepper. Cook 8 to 10 minutes or until you begin to see caramelized flecks throughout cauliflower, stirring occasionally. If desired, sprinkle cauliflower with cilantro and additional orange zest. Serve with chicken thighs.

PER SERVING *(1 chicken thigh + ⅓ cup cauliflower rice each)* **CAL** 285, **FAT** 13 g (3 g sat. fat), **CHOL** 145 mg, **SODIUM** 526 mg, **CARB** 9 g (2 g fiber, 5 g sugars), **PRO** 32 g

Orange Chicken Thighs with Cauliflower Rice

Jerk Marinated Chicken with Caribbean Rice

29 g
CARB

SERVES 4
HANDS ON 25 min.
TOTAL 6 hr. 40 min.

2 8-oz. skinless, boneless chicken breast halves
2 Tbsp. canola oil
2 Tbsp. red wine vinegar
2 Tbsp. orange juice
2 Tbsp. thinly sliced green onion

1 Tbsp. packed brown sugar
1 Tbsp. reduced-sodium soy sauce
1 Tbsp. finely chopped fresh jalapeño chile pepper, seeded (tip, p. 154)
2 tsp. Caribbean jerk seasoning
3 cloves garlic, minced
⅛ tsp. salt
1 recipe Caribbean Rice
   Lime wedges

1. Place chicken in a resealable plastic bag set in a shallow dish. For marinade, in a small bowl stir together the next 10 ingredients (through salt). Pour marinade over chicken. Seal bag; turn to coat chicken. Marinate in the refrigerator 6 to 24 hours, turning bag occasionally.

2. Drain chicken, reserving marinade. Grill chicken, covered, over medium 15 to 18 minutes or until done (165°F), turning once. Remove from grill and let stand 5 minutes.

3. Meanwhile, for glaze, in a small saucepan bring the reserved marinade to boiling; reduce heat. Simmer, uncovered, about 10 minutes or until reduced to ¼ cup. Slice chicken. Serve over Caribbean Rice with lime wedges; drizzle with glaze.

Caribbean Rice Coat an 8-inch nonstick skillet with **nonstick cooking spray**; heat over medium-high. Add **½ cup each chopped fresh pineapple and chopped green sweet pepper; 1 Tbsp. finely chopped fresh jalapeño chile pepper, seeded if desired (tip, p. 154); ¼ tsp. each salt, garlic powder, and black pepper;** and **⅛ tsp. ground cinnamon.** Cook 5 minutes, stirring occasionally. Stir in **one 8.8-oz. pouch cooked whole grain brown rice, ½ cup canned no-salt-added red kidney beans,** and **¼ cup orange juice**; heat through. Stir in **¼ cup snipped fresh cilantro.**

PER SERVING (3 oz. chicken + ¾ cup rice + 1 Tbsp. glaze each) **CAL** 286, **FAT** 6 g (1 g sat. fat), **CHOL** 83 mg, **SODIUM** 265 mg, **CARB** 29 g (5 g fiber, 5 g sugars), **PRO** 30 g

Jerk Marinated Chicken with Caribbean Rice

Chicken Pasta Primavera

45 g CARB

SERVES 2
HANDS ON 40 min.
TOTAL 50 min.

- 2 tsp. olive oil
- ¼ cup chopped onion
- 1 clove garlic, minced
- 2 cups cauliflower florets
- ½ cup reduced-sodium chicken broth
- ¼ cup water
- 3 Tbsp. finely shredded Parmesan cheese
- ⅛ tsp. salt
- ⅛ tsp. black pepper
- 3 oz. dried whole grain spaghetti or linguine
- 2 cups broccoli florets, 1-inch asparagus pieces, and/or coarsely chopped yellow summer squash
- ¾ cup bite-size strips red sweet pepper

Nonstick cooking spray
- 4 chicken breast tenderloins (8 oz. total), halved crosswise
- 2 Tbsp. snipped fresh basil
Lemon zest (optional)

1. For sauce, in a small saucepan heat oil over medium. Add onion and garlic; cook 3 to 4 minutes or until onion is tender, stirring occasionally. Stir in cauliflower and broth. Bring to boiling; reduce heat. Simmer, covered, about 15 minutes or until tender; cool slightly. Transfer to a food processor. Add the water, cheese, salt, and black pepper. Cover and process until smooth.

2. Meanwhile, cook pasta according to package directions, adding broccoli and sweet pepper the last 5 minutes. Drain, reserving ¼ cup of the pasta cooking water.

3. Coat a 10-inch skillet with cooking spray; heat over medium. Add chicken; cook about 10 minutes or until done (165°F), turning once. Stir in sauce and pasta mixture. Heat through, stirring in enough of the reserved pasta cooking water if needed to reach desired consistency. Serve topped with basil and, if desired, lemon zest and additional cheese.

For 4 To serve four, double ingredient amounts and use a 2-qt. saucepan and 12-inch skillet.

PER SERVING *(2 cups each)* **CAL** 451, **FAT** 12 g (3 g sat. fat), **CHOL** 88 mg, **SODIUM** 527 mg, **CARB** 45 g (9 g fiber, 9 g sugars), **PRO** 42 g

Spicy Chicken
Tostadas with
Charred Corn

Spicy Chicken Tostadas with Charred Corn

23 g CARB

SERVES 4
TOTAL 30 min.

- 8 oz. shredded cooked chicken
- 1 tsp. salt-free Southwest chipotle seasoning
- ⅛ tsp. salt
- ¼ cup plain fat-free Greek yogurt
- 2 Tbsp. snipped fresh cilantro
- 1 tsp. lime juice
- 1 cup frozen fire-roasted corn or whole kernel corn, thawed
- 1 cup packaged shredded coleslaw mix or finely shredded cabbage
- ½ of a small jalapeño pepper, seeded and finely chopped (tip, p. 154)
- 1 medium avocado, halved, seeded, peeled, and mashed
- 4 tostada shells
- ½ cup halved and/or quartered cherry tomatoes
- ¼ cup crumbled Cotija cheese or shredded reduced-fat Monterey Jack cheese (1 oz.) Lime wedges

1. In a bowl combine chicken, chipotle seasoning, and salt; toss to coat.
2. For corn slaw, in a medium bowl stir together yogurt, cilantro, and the lime juice. Add corn, coleslaw mix, and jalapeño pepper; mix well.
3. Spread avocado on tostada shells. Top with chicken, the corn slaw, tomatoes, cheese, and additional cilantro leaves. Serve with lime wedges.

PER SERVING (1 tostada each) **CAL** 272, **FAT** 15 g (4 g sat. fat), **CHOL** 59 mg, **SODIUM** 321 mg, **CARB** 23 g (5 g fiber, 4 g sugars), **PRO** 23 g

Chicken Caesar Flatbreads

Chicken Caesar Flatbreads

16 g CARB

SERVES 4
HANDS ON 15 min.
TOTAL 25 min.

- 2 rustic white or spicy Italian artisan pizza thin-crust flatbreads, such as Flatout brand
- 3 Tbsp. light sour cream
- 3 Tbsp. light Caesar dressing
- 1 cup shredded cooked chicken breast
- 1 cup shredded part-skim mozzarella cheese (4 oz.)
- 2 cups chopped romaine lettuce
- ½ cup quartered cherry tomatoes
- ¼ cup finely shredded Parmesan cheese
- 2 slices lower-sodium, less-fat bacon, cooked and crumbled

1. Preheat oven to 450°F. Cut pizza crusts in half crosswise. Place crusts on a large baking sheet. Bake 4 minutes.
2. In a bowl stir together sour cream and dressing. Spread 3 Tbsp. of the mixture over flatbreads. Top with chicken and mozzarella. Bake 3 to 5 minutes more or until cheese is melted and crust is golden brown.
3. Meanwhile, in a bowl toss romaine with remaining 2 Tbsp. sour cream mixture. Top flatbreads with romaine and sprinkle with tomatoes, Parmesan cheese, and bacon.

Tip Use flatbread with no more than 25 g carbohydrate and 250 mg sodium per flatbread, such as Flatout brand.

PER SERVING (½ flatbread each) **CAL** 255, **FAT** 10 g (5 g sat. fat), **CHOL** 56 mg, **SODIUM** 534 mg, **CARB** 16 g (2 g fiber, 3 g sugars), **PRO** 25 g

Chicken Sausage and Peppers

20 g CARB

SERVES 4
HANDS ON 15 min.
TOTAL 55 min.

Nonstick cooking spray
4 medium red, yellow, orange, and/or green sweet peppers, cut into 1-inch pieces
1 large sweet onion, cut into wedges
2 cups grape tomatoes
1 Tbsp. olive oil
1 Tbsp. balsamic vinegar
1 12-oz. pkg. Italian-flavor cooked chicken sausage, bias-sliced into thirds
1 Tbsp. snipped fresh oregano
Toasted baguette slices (optional)

1. Preheat oven to 425°F. Coat a 15×10-inch baking pan with cooking spray. In prepared pan combine peppers, onion, and tomatoes. Drizzle with olive oil and balsamic vinegar; toss gently to coat. Roast 30 minutes.
2. Push vegetables to one side, exposing about one-fourth of the pan. Place sausages in pan. Roast 10 to 15 minutes more or until vegetables are tender and sausage is heated. Sprinkle with oregano. If desired, serve with toasted baguette slices.

For 2 To serve two, cut ingredient amounts in half and use a 13×9-inch baking pan.

To Make Ahead Cut up the vegetables and place in a resealable plastic bag; seal bag. Refrigerate up to 24 hours.

PER SERVING *(1⅓ cups each)* **CAL** 249, **FAT** 11 g (3 g sat. fat), **CHOL** 65 mg, **SODIUM** 494 mg, **CARB** 20 g (5 g fiber, 11 g sugars), **PRO** 18 g

Chicken Sausage and Peppers

Turkey-Pepper Popper Casserole

34 g **CARB**

SERVES 6
HANDS ON 30 min.
TOTAL 1 hr. 5 min.

Nonstick cooking spray
6 oz. dried multigrain spaghetti, broken in half

2 tsp. olive oil
2 cups chopped red and/or green sweet peppers
1 cup thin bite-size slices fresh poblano chile pepper, seeded if desired (tip, p. 154)
1 to 2 fresh jalapeño peppers, halved, seeded (if desired), and thinly sliced (tip, p. 154)

2 cloves garlic, minced
2 Tbsp. all-purpose flour
½ tsp. salt
1 cup evaporated low-fat milk
½ cup unsalted chicken broth
1 cup shredded reduced-fat cheddar cheese (4 oz.)
3 oz. reduced-fat cream cheese (neufchatel), cut up, softened

Turkey-Pepper Popper Casserole

2 cups chopped cooked turkey breast (12 oz.)

⅓ cup whole wheat panko bread crumbs

1. Preheat oven to 375°F. Coat a 1½-qt. gratin dish or baking dish with cooking spray. Cook spaghetti according to package directions. Drain, reserving 1 cup of the cooking water.

2. Meanwhile, in a 12-inch nonstick skillet heat oil over medium-high. Add all peppers and the garlic; cook and stir 4 minutes. Sprinkle flour and salt over peppers; cook and stir 2 minutes. Add evaporated milk and broth; cook and stir about 5 minutes or until boiling and slightly thickened.

3. Remove skillet from heat. Add cheeses, stirring until melted. Add turkey and cooked spaghetti. Stir in enough of the reserved cooking water, ¼ cup at a time, to make desired consistency. Transfer to prepared baking dish. Sprinkle with panko; coat with cooking spray.

4. Bake 25 to 30 minutes or until edges are bubbly and top is browned. Remove from oven. Let stand 5 minutes before serving.

PER SERVING *(1 cup each)* **CAL** 358, **FAT** 12 g (5 g sat. fat), **CHOL** 70 mg, **SODIUM** 537 mg, **CARB** 34 g (4 g fiber, 8 g sugars), **PRO** 32 g

Eggplant-Turkey Pasta Bake

Eggplant-Turkey Pasta Bake

33 g
CARB

SERVES 4
HANDS ON 25 min.
TOTAL 45 min.

Nonstick cooking spray

4 oz. whole grain medium shells or penne pasta

1 cup light Alfredo pasta sauce

8 oz. lean ground turkey

½ of a 1-lb. eggplant, peeled if desired and cut into ½-inch cubes (4 cups)

½ cup + 1 Tbsp. chopped red onion

3 cloves garlic, minced

1½ cups chopped roma tomatoes

2 tsp. dried Italian seasoning, crushed

1 tsp. fennel seeds, crushed

½ cup shredded part-skim mozzarella cheese (2 oz.)

2 Tbsp. snipped fresh basil

⅛ tsp. black pepper

1. Preheat oven to 400°F. Coat four individual 10- to 12-oz. casseroles or ramekins with cooking spray. Cook pasta according to package directions. Drain, reserving ½ cup pasta cooking water; return pasta to pot. Stir in half of the Alfredo sauce and enough of the reserved cooking water to make creamy.

2. Meanwhile, in a 10-inch nonstick skillet cook turkey, eggplant, ½ cup of the onion, and the garlic over medium-high until turkey is no longer pink, stirring occasionally. Stir in 1 cup of the chopped tomatoes, the Italian seasoning, and fennel seeds. Cover and cook 3 minutes. Stir in remaining Alfredo sauce.

3. Spoon half of the eggplant mixture into the prepared casseroles. Top with half of the pasta mixture. Repeat layers.

4. Bake casseroles, covered, 15 to 20 minutes or until heated through. Uncover; sprinkle with cheese. Bake about 5 minutes more or until cheese is melted.

5. In a bowl toss together the remaining ½ cup tomatoes and 1 Tbsp. red onion, the basil, and pepper. Spoon over baked pasta.

PER SERVING *(1 individual casserole each)* **CAL** 321, **FAT** 13 g (6 g sat. fat), **CHOL** 76 mg, **SODIUM** 467 mg, **CARB** 33 g (6 g fiber, 7 g sugars), **PRO** 20 g

**Skillet Steaks
with Mushrooms**

Skillet Steaks with Mushrooms

8 g
CARB

SERVES	4
TOTAL	30 min.

- 2 8-oz. boneless beef top loin steaks, cut ¾ to 1 inch thick and trimmed of fat
- ½ tsp. cracked black pepper
- ¼ tsp. sea salt
- 1 tsp. olive oil
- 8 oz. fresh mushrooms, quartered
- 1 cup frozen small whole onions
- 4 cloves garlic, minced
- ¾ cup dry red wine
- 1 cup reduced-sodium beef broth
- 2½ tsp. cornstarch or arrowroot Fresh parsley (optional)

1. Sprinkle steaks with pepper and salt. In a 10-inch skillet heat oil over medium-high. Reduce heat to medium. Add steaks; cook 8 to 10 minutes or until medium rare (145°F), turning once. Remove from skillet; cover and keep warm.

2. For sauce, in skillet cook mushrooms and onions over medium-high about 5 minutes or until tender, stirring frequently. Add garlic; cook and stir 1 minute. Carefully add wine. Boil gently, uncovered, 5 minutes, stirring occasionally. In a bowl stir together broth and cornstarch; stir into mushroom mixture. Cook and stir until thickened and bubbly. Cook and stir 1 minute more.

3. Cut steaks in half and return to skillet; heat through, turning to coat with sauce. If desired, top with parsley.

PER SERVING *(3 oz. cooked meat + ⅔ cup sauce each)* **CAL** 267, **FAT** 11 g (4 g sat. fat), **CHOL** 69 mg, **SODIUM** 306 mg, **CARB** 8 g (1 g fiber, 3 g sugars), **PRO** 28 g

Loaded Taco Sweet Potatoes

31 g
CARB

SERVES	4
HANDS ON	30 min.
TOTAL	1 hr. 20 min.

- 2 8- to 10-oz. sweet potatoes
- 8 oz. extra-lean ground beef
- 1 small onion, halved and sliced
- 1 small fresh poblano chile pepper, seeded and cut into bite-size strips (tip, *p. 154*)
- ½ cup salsa
- 1 tsp. chili powder
- ¼ cup crumbled queso fresco or shredded reduced-fat cheddar cheese (1 oz.)
- ¼ cup light sour cream Toppers: slivered red onion or sliced green onions, fresh cilantro, quartered grape tomatoes, sliced fresh jalapeno chiles (tip, *p. 154*), and/or chopped avocado

1. Preheat oven to 425°F. Scrub potatoes; pat dry. Pierce potatoes with a fork. Wrap potatoes individually in foil and place in a 15×10-inch baking pan. Bake 50 to 60 minutes or until tender.

2. Meanwhile, in a 10-inch nonstick skillet cook beef, onion, and poblano chile about 6 minutes or until beef is browned and vegetables are tender. Remove from heat; drain any fat. Add salsa and chili powder; toss to combine.

3. Cut baked sweet potatoes in half lengthwise. Scrape pulp with a fork to loosen. Top with beef mixture, cheese, and sour cream. Add desired toppers.

PER SERVING *(1 loaded sweet potato half each)* **CAL** 272, **FAT** 10 g (4 g sat. fat), **CHOL** 45 mg, **SODIUM** 417 mg, **CARB** 31 g (6 g fiber, 8 g sugars), **PRO** 17 g

Loaded Taco Sweet Potatoes

**Bulgogi Beef and
Vegetable Bowls**

Bulgogi Beef and Vegetable Bowls

43 g CARB

SERVES 4	
HANDS ON 35 min.	
TOTAL 4 hr. 35 min.	

- 1 lb. boneless beef sirloin steak, cut 1 inch thick
- ½ cup coarsely chopped onion
- ¼ cup honey
- ¼ cup water
- 2 Tbsp. reduced-sodium soy sauce
- 2 Tbsp. toasted sesame oil
- 1 Tbsp. finely chopped fresh ginger
- 4 cloves garlic, halved
  Nonstick cooking spray
- 1⅓ cups cooked brown rice
- 1 cup coarsely shredded carrots
- 1 cup finely shredded red cabbage
- ¾ cup cooked small broccoli florets
- ½ cup coarsely shredded cucumber
- ¼ cup snipped fresh cilantro or mint
- 1 to 2 tsp. sriracha sauce
- ½ cup kimchi (optional)

1. Trim fat from meat. Cut meat across the grain into very thin slices. Place meat in a resealable plastic bag set in a shallow dish. For marinade, in a blender or food processor combine onion, 2 Tbsp. each of the honey and water, the soy sauce, 1 Tbsp. of the sesame oil, the ginger, and garlic. Cover and blend or process until smooth. Pour marinade over meat. Seal bag; turn to coat meat. Marinate in the refrigerator 4 to 6 hours, turning bag occasionally.

2. Drain meat, discarding marinade. Coat a 12-inch grill pan or nonstick skillet with cooking spray; heat over medium-high. Working in batches, add meat; cook and stir 40 to 60 seconds or just until slightly pink in center.

3. To assemble, divide meat and the next five ingredients (through cucumber) among shallow bowls,

QUICK TIP
For easier slicing, partially freeze the meat.

keeping ingredients in separate piles. In a small bowl stir together the remaining 2 Tbsp. each honey and water, the remaining 1 Tbsp. sesame oil, the cilantro, and sriracha sauce. Top bowls with honey mixture and, if desired, kimchi and additional cilantro or mint.

For 2 To serve two, cut the recipe in half. Rather than cook such a small amount of rice, however, look for frozen cooked rice and prepare it as directed on the package or use leftovers saved from another meal.

Tip To cook rice, in a small saucepan bring ⅔ cup water and ⅓ cup uncooked long grain brown rice to boiling; reduce heat. Simmer, covered, 35 to 45 minutes or until rice is tender and liquid is absorbed.

PER SERVING *(1 bowl each)* **CAL** 397, **FAT** 13 g (3 g sat. fat), **CHOL** 77 mg, **SODIUM** 435 mg, **CARB** 43 g (3 g fiber, 23 g sugars), **PRO** 30 g

Hot Beef Sundaes

Hot Beef Sundaes

22 g
CARB

SERVES 4
HANDS ON 20 min.
TOTAL 1 hr. 25 min.

Nonstick cooking spray
1 lb. beef stew meat, trimmed of fat
1 14.5-oz. can reduced-sodium beef broth
3 cloves garlic, minced
¼ tsp. black pepper
2 cups cubed, peeled russet potatoes
2 cups small cauliflower florets
1 Tbsp. olive oil
¼ tsp. salt
⅛ tsp. black pepper
2 to 4 Tbsp. fat-free milk
¼ cup cold water
2 Tbsp. all-purpose flour
¼ cup shredded reduced-fat cheddar cheese (1 oz.)
¼ cup chopped green onions
4 cherry tomatoes

1. Coat a medium saucepan with cooking spray. Brown the stew meat, half at a time, over medium-high. Return all beef to pan. Add broth, 2 cloves of the garlic, and the ¼ tsp. pepper. Bring to boiling; reduce heat. Simmer, covered, about 1 hour or until very tender. Using a slotted spoon, remove meat from pan. Shred beef using two forks.

2. Meanwhile, in another medium saucepan combine potatoes and the remaining 1 clove garlic. Add enough water to cover by 1 inch. Bring to boiling; reduce heat. Simmer, covered, 5 minutes. Add cauliflower; return to boiling. Reduce heat. Simmer, covered, about 10 minutes more or until vegetables are very tender. Drain well.

3. In a bowl combine potato-cauliflower mixture, oil, salt, and the ⅛ tsp. pepper. Mash mixture. Gradually stir in enough milk to make mixture light and fluffy.

4. If desired, strain beef cooking liquid through a fine-mesh sieve. Measure 1 cup liquid; return to pan. In a bowl stir together cold water and flour until smooth. Stir into cooking liquid in pan. Cook and stir over medium until thickened and bubbly; cook and stir 1 minute more. Return shredded meat to pan; stir to combine.

5. To serve, scoop potato-cauliflower mash into bowls. Top with beef mixture, cheese, green onions, and tomatoes.

PER SERVING *(1 cup each)* **CAL** 298, **FAT** 10 g (4 g sat. fat), **CHOL** 78 mg, **SODIUM** 489 mg, **CARB** 22 g (2 g fiber, 3 g sugars), **PRO** 31 g

Moroccan-Spiced
Pot Roast and Veggies

Moroccan-Spiced Pot Roast and Veggies

37 g CARB

SERVES 6
HANDS ON 30 min.
SLOW COOK 9 hr. 30 min.

- 2 tsp. pumpkin pie spice
- 1 tsp. kosher salt
- 1 tsp. ground cumin
- ½ tsp. black pepper
- ⅛ tsp. cayenne pepper (optional)
- 1 2½-lb. boneless beef chuck arm pot roast, trimmed of fat
- 1 Tbsp. olive oil
- 1¼ lb. carrots, cut into 1-inch pieces
- 3 cups 1-inch pieces peeled parsnips
- 2 large onions, cut into wedges
- 1 cup reduced-sodium beef broth
- 3 Tbsp. quick-cooking tapioca, crushed
- 2 Tbsp. no-salt-added tomato paste
- ½ tsp. dry mustard
- 2 medium red sweet peppers, seeded and cut into 1-inch pieces
  Snipped fresh cilantro (optional)

1. In a bowl combine pumpkin pie spice, ½ tsp. of the salt, the cumin, ¼ tsp. of the black pepper, and, if desired, cayenne pepper. Sprinkle mixture over meat; rub in with your fingers. In a 10-inch skillet heat oil over medium-high. Add meat; cook 6 to 8 minutes or until browned on all sides.
2. In a 5- to 6-qt. slow cooker combine carrots and parsnips. Add meat, cutting to fit if needed. Top with onions. In a bowl stir together broth, tapioca, tomato paste, dry mustard, and remaining ½ tsp. salt and ¼ tsp. black pepper. Pour over mixture in cooker.
3. Cover and cook on low 9 hours or high 4½ hours. If slow cooker is on low, turn to high. Add sweet peppers. Cover and cook 30 minutes more.
4. Using a slotted spoon, transfer meat and vegetables to a platter. Skim fat from cooking liquid. Drizzle cooking liquid over meat and vegetables. If desired, sprinkle with cilantro.

PER SERVING (3⅔ oz. meat + 1⅓ cups veggies each) **CAL** 430, **FAT** 11 g (3 g sat. fat), **CHOL** 123 mg, **SODIUM** 473 mg, **CARB** 37 g (9 g fiber, 13 g sugars), **PRO** 45 g

Slow-Cooked Pork Tacos with Chipotle Aïoli

Slow-Cooked Pork Tacos with Chipotle Aïoli

36 g CARB

SERVES 4
HANDS ON 40 min.
SLOW COOK 7 hr.

- 2½ cups Shredded Seasoned Pork
- 1 cup shredded romaine lettuce
- 1 cup chopped mango
- ⅔ cup thin bite-size strips, peeled jicama
- ½ cup light mayonnaise
- 2 Tbsp. lime juice
- 2 cloves garlic, minced
- ½ to 1 tsp. finely chopped canned chipotle pepper in adobo sauce or ¼ tsp. ground chipotle chile pepper
- 8 6-inch corn tortillas, warmed
- ¼ cup snipped fresh cilantro

1. Prepare Shredded Seasoned Pork. In a bowl combine lettuce, mango, and jicama. For chipotle aïoli, in a small bowl stir together the next four ingredients (through chipotle pepper).
2. Serve shredded meat, lettuce mixture, and chipotle aïoli in tortillas; sprinkle with cilantro.

Shredded Seasoned Pork Trim fat from **one 2- to 2½-lb. boneless pork sirloin roast.** Sprinkle with **3 Tbsp. reduced-sodium taco seasoning mix;** rub in with your fingers. Place meat in a 3½- or 4-qt. slow cooker. Add **one 14.5-oz. can no-salt-added diced tomatoes, undrained.** Cover and cook on low 7 to 8 hours or high 3½ to 4 hours. Remove meat, reserving cooking liquid. Shred meat using two forks. Toss meat with enough cooking liquid to moisten. Makes about 5 cups.

PER SERVING (2 tacos each) **CAL** 325, **FAT** 11 g (2 g sat. fat), **CHOL** 57 mg, **SODIUM** 451 mg, **CARB** 36 g (6 g fiber, 10 g sugars), **PRO** 20 g

Asian Pork Nachos with Wasabi Cream

29 g
CARB

SERVES 4	
HANDS ON 15 min.	
TOTAL 30 min.	

- 12 6-inch extra-thin corn tortillas
  Nonstick cooking spray
- 6 oz. shredded cooked pork loin
  or chicken breast
- 1 Tbsp. reduced-sodium
  soy sauce
- ½ tsp. Chinese five-spice powder
- 2 Tbsp. light sour cream
- 2 Tbsp. plain fat-free Greek
  yogurt
- 2 tsp. water
- ½ tsp. prepared wasabi paste
- 1 cup shredded reduced-fat
  cheddar cheese (4 oz.)
- 2 cups packaged shredded
  cabbage with carrot
  (coleslaw mix)
- ¼ cup sliced green onions
- ¼ cup snipped fresh cilantro

1. Preheat oven to 425°F. Cut each
tortilla into six wedges. Arrange
wedges, one-third at a time, in a
15×10-inch baking pan; lightly coat
with cooking spray. Bake about
8 minutes or until golden and crisp.
2. In a bowl combine shredded meat,
soy sauce, and five-spice powder.
For wasabi cream, in another bowl stir
together the next four ingredients
(through wasabi paste).
3. Spread all of the baked tortilla
wedges in the baking pan. Top with
meat mixture and sprinkle with
cheese. Bake about 5 minutes or until
cheese is melted.
4. Top nachos with coleslaw mix,
green onions, and cilantro. Drizzle
with wasabi cream.

For 2 To serve two, cut ingredient
amounts in half and use a 13×9-inch
baking pan.

PER SERVING *(18 tortilla wedges + toppings
each)* **CAL** 325, **FAT** 13 g (6 g sat. fat),
CHOL 58 mg, **SODIUM** 425 mg, **CARB** 29 g
(4 g fiber, 4 g sugars), **PRO** 24 g

QUICK TIP Don't have
wasabi paste? Use 1 tsp
sriracha sauce and omit
the water.

Asian Pork Nachos
with Wasabi Cream

Corn-Crusted Fish and
Sweet Potato Wedges

Corn-Crusted Fish and Sweet Potato Wedges

40 g
CARB

| SERVES 4 |
| HANDS ON 25 min. |
| TOTAL 50 min. |

4 4-oz. fresh or frozen white fish
fillets, such as haddock, cod,
catfish, or mahi mahi, about
1 inch thick
½ cup plain fat-free Greek yogurt
¼ cup sliced green onions
2 tsp. lime juice
1 tsp. kosher salt
½ tsp. black pepper
3 cups packaged shredded
cabbage with carrot
(coleslaw mix)
Nonstick cooking spray
1 lb. sweet potatoes, cut into
½-inch wedges
2 Tbsp. olive oil
1 tsp. chili powder
1 egg, lightly beaten
1 Tbsp. water
2½ cups puffed corn cereal or corn
flakes, coarsely crushed
Lime wedges

1. Preheat oven to 400°F. Thaw fish, if frozen. For slaw, in a medium bowl stir together yogurt, green onions, lime juice, ½ tsp. of the salt, and ¼ tsp. of the pepper. Stir in coleslaw mix. Cover and chill until ready to serve.
2. Line a 15×10-inch baking pan with foil; lightly coat with cooking spray. Place sweet potatoes in the prepared pan. Drizzle with 1 Tbsp. of the oil and sprinkle with ¼ tsp. of the salt and the chili powder; toss to coat. Bake 20 to 25 minutes or until tender and browned.

3. Meanwhile, rinse fish; pat dry. In a shallow dish combine egg and the water. In another shallow dish combine crushed cereal and the remaining ¼ tsp. salt and ¼ tsp. pepper. Dip fish in egg mixture, then in cereal mixture, turning to coat.
4. In a 10-inch oven-going skillet heat the remaining 1 Tbsp. oil over medium-high. Add fish; cook just until browned. Turn fish. Transfer skillet to oven. Bake 14 to 16 minutes or until fish flakes easily. Serve fish with sweet potatoes, slaw, and lime wedges.

PER SERVING *(1 fish fillet + 8 potato wedges + ½ cup slaw each)* **CAL** 366,
FAT 10 g (2 g sat. fat), **CHOL** 103 mg,
SODIUM 564 mg, **CARB** 40 g (6 g fiber,
9 g sugars), **PRO** 29 g

Seafood Boil

28 g CARB

SERVES 6
HANDS ON 30 min.
TOTAL 40 min.

8 oz. fresh or frozen shrimp in shells
8 oz. fresh or frozen skinless salmon fillets
2 Tbsp. olive oil
3 oz. cooked Italian-style chicken sausage, halved lengthwise and sliced ½ inch thick
1½ cups sliced celery
1 cup coarsely chopped red onion
1 cup water
1 cup dry white wine or ¾ cup reduced-sodium chicken broth + 2 Tbsp. white wine vinegar
2 sprigs fresh parsley
1 tsp. celery seeds
½ tsp. paprika
½ tsp. black pepper
¼ tsp. kosher salt
¼ tsp. cayenne pepper
12 live clams in shells, scrubbed and soaked
2 large ears of corn, each cut into 3 chunks
3 tablespoons snipped fresh parsley
6 1-oz. slices French bread, toasted

1. Thaw shrimp and salmon, if frozen. Devein shrimp, but do not peel. Rinse shrimp and salmon; pat dry. Cut salmon into six pieces.
2. In a 5-qt. Dutch oven heat oil over medium. Add sausage; cook and stir 3 minutes or until browned. Add celery and onion; cook about 5 minutes or just until tender, stirring occasionally.
3. Stir in the next eight ingredients (through cayenne pepper). Bring to boiling. Add clams and corn. Return to boiling; reduce heat. Simmer, covered, 4 minutes. Stir in shrimp and salmon. Simmer, covered, 4 to 5 minutes more or until clam shells open, shrimp are opaque, and salmon flakes easily. Discard any clams that do not open.
4. Top servings with parsley and serve with toasted bread.

Tip To clean live clams, scrub clams in shells under cold running water. In a large container stir together 8 cups cold water and 2½ Tbsp. salt; add clams. Soak 15 minutes; drain and rinse. Discard water. Repeat soaking, draining, and rinsing twice.

PER SERVING (2 cups each) **CAL** 334, **FAT** 10 g (2 g sat. fat), **CHOL** 101 mg, **SODIUM** 566 mg, **CARB** 28 g (3 g fiber, 6 g sugars), **PRO** 27 g

QUICK TIP You have to use your fingers to peel shrimp and hold clams to get at the meat. Have lots of napkins on hand. Use the bread to soak up every drop of broth.

Grilled Asparagus and Shrimp with Pasta

38 g CARB | **SERVES** 4
TOTAL 45 min.

16 fresh or frozen jumbo or extra-large shrimp in shells (about 1 lb.)

6 oz. dried whole grain linguine
1 lemon
2 Tbsp. olive oil
½ cup chopped onion
½ tsp. black pepper
½ cup finely shredded Parmesan cheese (2 oz.)
½ cup reduced-sodium chicken broth

1 Tbsp. butter
3 cloves garlic, minced
12 oz. fresh asparagus, trimmed
Nonstick cooking spray
2 Tbsp. snipped fresh mint

1. Thaw shrimp, if frozen. If using wooden skewers, soak in water

Grilled Asparagus and Shrimp with Pasta

30 minutes; drain. Peel and devein shrimp, leaving tails intact if desired. Rinse shrimp; pat dry. Cook linguine in a large amount of boiling water 6 minutes. Drain, reserving ⅔ cup of the pasta cooking water. Keep warm.

2. Meanwhile, remove 1 tsp. zest and squeeze 1 Tbsp. juice from lemon. In a 10-inch skillet heat 1 Tbsp. of the oil over medium. Add onion; cook 4 minutes, stirring occasionally. Add linguine, the reserved pasta cooking water, and ¼ tsp. of the pepper. Cook about 4 minutes or just until pasta is tender and most of the water is absorbed, stirring frequently. Add lemon juice, ¼ cup of the cheese, the broth, and butter. Cook and stir 2 minutes more.

3. In a bowl combine shrimp, the remaining 1 Tbsp. oil and ¼ tsp. pepper, and the garlic. Thread shrimp onto four 10-inch skewers, leaving ¼ inch between pieces. Coat asparagus with cooking spray.

4. Grill shrimp skewers and asparagus (place across the grates), covered, over medium 4 to 6 minutes or until shrimp are opaque and asparagus is crisp-tender, turning once.

5. Cut tips from asparagus; cut stalks into 1-inch pieces. Stir asparagus into linguine mixture; heat through. Top linguine mixture with shrimp skewers, the remaining ¼ cup cheese, lemon zest, and mint.

PER SERVING (4 shrimp + 1¼ cups pasta mixture each) **CAL** 397, **FAT** 14 g (5 g sat. fat), **CHOL** 174 mg, **SODIUM** 385 mg, **CARB** 38 g (7 g fiber, 4 g sugars), **PRO** 32 g

Seared Scallops with Roasted Red Pepper Sauce and Succotash

29 g
CARB

SERVES 4
HANDS ON 25 min.
TOTAL 50 min.

- 2 medium red sweet peppers
- 8 fresh or frozen sea scallops (about 1 lb.)
- 3 Tbsp. lemon juice
- 3 Tbsp. olive oil

Seared Scallops with Roasted Red Pepper Sauce and Succotash

- 2 cloves garlic, minced
- ¾ tsp. kosher salt
- ½ tsp. black pepper
  Nonstick cooking spray
- 1 cup frozen cut green beans, thawed
- 1 cup frozen baby lima beans, thawed
- ½ cup frozen edamame, thawed
- ½ cup frozen peas, thawed
- ½ cup frozen whole kernel corn, thawed
- 2 Tbsp. snipped fresh basil
  Lemon wedges

1. Preheat broiler. Cut sweet peppers in half lengthwise; remove stems, seeds, and membranes. Place peppers, cut sides down, on a foil-lined baking sheet. Broil 6 inches from heat 10 to 12 minutes or until well charred. Bring foil up around peppers and fold edges together to enclose. Let stand 15 to 20 minutes or until cool enough to handle. Peel off and discard skins.

2. Meanwhile, thaw scallops, if frozen. For vinaigrette, in a screw-top jar combine lemon juice, 2 Tbsp. of the oil, the garlic, and ¼ tsp. each of the salt

and black pepper. Cover and shake well. For sauce, in a blender combine sweet peppers and 3 Tbsp. of the vinaigrette. Cover and blend until smooth.

3. For succotash, coat a 10-inch skillet with cooking spray; heat over medium-high. Add the next five ingredients (through corn). Cook 5 minutes, stirring occasionally. Stir in the remaining vinaigrette; heat through. Transfer to a bowl; cover to keep warm.

4. Rinse scallops; pat dry. Sprinkle with the remaining ½ tsp. salt and ¼ tsp. black pepper. In skillet heat the remaining 1 Tbsp. oil over medium-high. Add scallops; cook about 4 minutes or until opaque and browned, turning once. Serve scallops on sauce with succotash, basil, and lemon wedges.

PER SERVING (2 scallops + ⅔ cup succotash + ¼ cup sauce each) **CAL** 340, **FAT** 13 g (2 g sat. fat), **CHOL** 37 mg, **SODIUM** 439 mg, **CARB** 29 g (7 g fiber, 6 g sugars), **PRO** 27 g

Avocado and Yogurt
Pasta Sauce with Veggies

¼ cup salsa
¼ cup Cashew Cream or sour
cream
Lime wedges (optional)
Optional toppings: toasted
pepitas, snipped fresh cilantro,
chopped avocado, salsa,
crumbled queso fresco, and
sliced green onions (optional)

1. Preheat oven to 425°F. In a medium
saucepan bring broth to boiling. Add
rice. Return to boiling; reduce heat.
Simmer, covered, about 45 minutes
or until rice is tender and broth is
absorbed. When rice is done, fluff
with fork and stir in cilantro and
green onion.
2. Meanwhile, on a foil-lined
15×10-inch baking pan combine the
next five ingredients (through salt);
toss to coat. Spread in a single layer.
Roast about 30 minutes or until slightly
browned and tender, stirring once.
3. In a bowl stir together the beans
and salsa.
4. Spoon rice into bowls. Top with
sweet potato mixture and bean
mixture. Drizzle with Cashew Cream
and, if desired, sprinkle with additional
chili powder. If desired, serve with lime
wedges and additional toppings.

Cashew Cream Place **1 cup raw
cashews** in a bowl and cover with
boiling water. Cover and let soak
30 minutes; drain. Place cashews in
a food processor with **½ cup water;
2 tsp. cider vinegar; 1 tsp. lime juice;
1 clove garlic, minced;** and **⅛ tsp.
salt.** Cover and process until smooth,
adding additional water as needed
make a smooth drizzling consistency.

Tip Burrito bowls can be assembled in
airtight containers and stored in the
refrigerator up to 3 days. Take for lunch
and enjoy bowls chilled.

PER SERVING (1¼ cups + toppings each)
CAL 349, **FAT** 9 g (1 g sat. fat), **CHOL** 0 mg,
SODIUM 465 mg, **CARB** 58 g (9 g fiber,
6 g sugars), **PRO** 10 g

Avocado and Yogurt Pasta Sauce with Veggies

29 g
CARB

| **SERVES** 4 |
| **TOTAL** 30 min. |

- 3 oz. dried whole grain spaghetti
- 1 ripe avocado, halved, seeded,
  and peeled
- 1 6-oz. carton plain fat-free
  Greek yogurt
- 2 Tbsp. lime juice
- ½ tsp. kosher salt
- ¼ to ½ tsp. sriracha sauce
- ¼ tsp. black pepper
- 1 Tbsp. olive oil
- ½ cup thinly sliced red onion
- 3 cloves garlic, minced
- 2 cups thin bite-size strips red
  and/or yellow sweet peppers
- 2 cups seeded and chopped
  cucumber
- ¼ cup snipped fresh cilantro

1. Cook spaghetti according to
package directions; drain and keep
warm. For sauce, in a bowl mash
avocado with a fork. Stir in the next five
ingredients (through black pepper).
2. In a 10-inch skillet heat oil over
medium. Add onion; cook 3 minutes,
stirring occasionally. Add garlic; cook
and stir 1 minute. Add sweet peppers;
cook 4 minutes more or until

vegetables are crisp-tender, stirring
occasionally. Remove from heat.
3. Stir in cucumber and yogurt
mixture. Cook over medium-low until
heated. Spoon sauce over cooked
spaghetti and top with cilantro.

PER SERVING (¾ cup sauce + ½ cup pasta
each) **CAL** 234, **FAT** 10 g (1 g sat. fat),
CHOL 0 mg, **SODIUM** 284 mg, **CARB** 29 g
(6 g fiber, 8 g sugars), **PRO** 10 g

Sweet Potato Burrito Bowls with Cashew Cream

58 g
CARB

| **SERVES** 4 |
| **HANDS ON** 30 min. |
| **TOTAL** 1 hr. 45 min. |

- 1½ cups no-salt-added vegetable
  stock or water
- ⅔ cup uncooked brown rice
- ¼ cup snipped fresh cilantro
- 2 Tbsp. sliced green onion
- 2 cups ¾-inch cubes peeled
  sweet potatoes
- 1 cup coarsely chopped red
  sweet pepper
- 1 Tbsp. olive oil
- 1 tsp. chili powder
- ¼ tsp. salt
- 1 15- to 16-oz. can no-salt-
  added pinto beans, rinsed and
  drained

**Sweet Potato Burrito Bowl
with Cashew Cream**

Lentil and Vegetable Bowl

42 g
CARB

SERVES 1
HANDS ON 10 min.
TOTAL 35 min.

- 2 oz. fresh green beans, trimmed
- 8 4×¼-inch carrot sticks
- ⅔ cup cooked brown lentils
- 1 Tbsp. snipped fresh parsley
- ½ tsp. lemon zest
- 1 cup mixed baby salad greens
- ¼ cup cherry or grape tomatoes, halved

- 1 hard-cooked egg, sliced
- 1 Tbsp. chopped toasted walnuts
- 1 recipe Lemon-Chive Aïoli

1. Place a steamer basket in a saucepan. Add water to just below bottom of the basket. Bring water to boiling. Add beans and carrots to steamer basket. Cover and reduce heat. Steam about 5 minutes or until crisp-tender. Carefully remove basket from pan and place in sink.

Rinse with cold water; drain well. Meanwhile, toss lentils with parsley and lemon zest.

2. In a bowl arrange lentil mixture and the next five ingredients (through egg). Sprinkle with walnuts. Top with Lemon-Chive Aïoli.

Lemon-Chive Aïoli In a bowl stir together **2 tsp. each reduced-fat sour cream, light mayonnaise, and snipped fresh chives; 1 tsp. lemon juice;** and a **dash black pepper.**

Lentil and Vegetable Bowl

Tip For cooked lentils, combine **2 cups reduced-sodium chicken broth** and **1 cup brown lentils, rinsed and drained**. Bring to boiling; reduce heat. Simmer, covered, 25 to 30 minutes or until tender. Drain if necessary. Yield is about 2⅓ cups cooked lentils. Store, covered, in an airtight container in the refrigerator up to 3 days.

To Tote Assemble salad in a covered container. Place Lemon-Chive Aïoli in a separate small container. Pack containers in an insulated bag with ice packs. To serve, top salad with aïoli.

For 2 To serve two, double ingredient amounts.

PER SERVING *(3 cups)* **CAL** 380, **FAT** 15 g (3 g sat. fat), **CHOL** 193 mg, **SODIUM** 184 mg, **CARB** 42 g (15 g fiber, 9 g sugars), **PRO** 22 g

Cauli-Rice and Smoky Black Bean Burger Stacks

Cauli-Rice and Smoky Black Bean Burger Stacks

36 g CARB

SERVES 4
HANDS ON 45 min.
TOTAL 1 hr. 15 min.

- 1 15-oz. can reduced-sodium black beans, rinsed and drained
- 1 egg, lightly beaten
- ½ cup finely chopped red sweet pepper
- ⅓ cup thinly sliced green onions
- ¼ cup yellow cornmeal
- 3 cloves garlic, minced
- 1 tsp. smoked paprika or regular paprika
  Nonstick cooking spray
- 3 cups cauliflower florets
- ¾ cup shredded Monterey Jack cheese (3 oz.)
- 1 egg, lightly beaten
- 2 cloves garlic, minced
- ½ cup refrigerated fresh salsa
- 1 avocado, halved, seeded, peeled, and chopped

1. In a large bowl combine half of the beans and 1 egg. Mash beans until nearly smooth. Stir in remaining beans and the next five ingredients (through paprika). Using damp hands, shape mixture into four ¾-inch-thick patties. Cover and chill at least 30 minutes or up to 8 hours.
2. Preheat oven to 375°F. Coat four 6-oz. custard cups with cooking spray. Place cauliflower in a food processor. Cover and process until very finely chopped. Transfer cauliflower to a large bowl. Add 2 Tbsp. water; cover with vented plastic wrap. Microwave 3 minutes, stirring once. Cool slightly; squeeze cauliflower with a double thickness of paper towels to absorb excess liquid.
3. In a bowl combine the cauliflower, cheese, 1 egg, and garlic; mix well.

Spoon cauliflower mixture into prepared custard cups, pressing with the back of a spoon. Bake 10 to 12 minutes or until done (160°F).
4. Coat a 10-inch nonstick skillet with cooking spray; heat over medium. Add bean patties. Cook 10 to 12 minutes or until done (160°F), turning once.
5. Place bean burgers on plates. Run a thin metal spatula or knife around edges of custard cups to loosen cauliflower rice. Invert the cauliflower rice on bean patties. Top with salsa and avocado.

PER SERVING *(1 burger + ⅓ cup cauli-rice + 2 Tbsp. salsa + ¼ avocado each)* **CAL** 344, **FAT** 15 g (6 g sat. fat), **CHOL** 112 mg, **SODIUM** 472 mg, **CARB** 36 g (9 g fiber, 5 g sugars), **PRO** 17 g

2

FRESH
SALAD MEALS

Get your daily dose of greens with a salad for lunch or dinner.

These garden-fresh meals have flavorful additions of meat,

seafood, or beans to provide the protein you need to keep

you satisfied. The salads are all complete meals, plus they are

easy to serve and quick to clean up.

QUICK TIP 〉〉
Use zucchini or
yellow summer
squash in place of
the cucumber.

**Chicken, Tomato,
and Cucumber Salad**

Chicken, Tomato, and Cucumber Salad

6 g
CARB

SERVES 4	
TOTAL 25 min.	

- 1 to 1¼ lb. chicken breast tenderloins
- ¼ tsp. salt
- ¼ tsp. black pepper
- 3 Tbsp. olive oil
- 3 Tbsp. cider vinegar or white wine vinegar
- 1½ tsp. snipped fresh thyme
- ½ tsp. sugar
- 1 medium cucumber, very thinly sliced
- 2 tomatoes, sliced
- ⅓ cup pitted green olives, halved and/or sliced
- 1 cup crumbled feta cheese (4 oz.) (optional)

1. Sprinkle chicken with ⅛ tsp. each of the salt and pepper. In a 10-inch skillet heat 1 Tbsp. of the oil over medium. Add chicken; cook 8 to 10 minutes or until no longer pink, turning once.
2. For vinaigrette, in a screw-top jar combine the remaining 2 Tbsp. oil, the vinegar, thyme, sugar, and the remaining ⅛ tsp. each salt and pepper. Cover and shake well.
3. In a large bowl combine chicken, cucumber, tomatoes, and olives. Add vinaigrette; toss gently to coat. If desired, sprinkle with cheese.

PER SERVING (3 oz. cooked chicken + ½ tomato + ¼ cup cucumber + 1½ Tbsp. olives each) **CAL** 267, **FAT** 15 g (2 g sat. fat), **CHOL** 83 mg, **SODIUM** 382 mg, **CARB** 6 g (1 g fiber, 3 g sugars), **PRO** 27 g

Southwest Kale Salad

Southwest Kale Salad

22 g
CARB

SERVES 4	
TOTAL 30 min.	

- 12 oz. Tuscan kale
- 12 oz. chopped cooked chicken or turkey
- ½ cup thinly sliced or thin bite-size strips carrot
- ½ cup red and/or yellow sweet pepper strips
- ⅓ cup fruit-juice sweetened dried cranberries
- ¼ cup pumpkin seeds (pepitas), toasted
- 2 limes
- 2 Tbsp. finely chopped shallot
- 2 Tbsp. olive oil
- 1 tsp. honey
- ½ tsp. salt
- ½ tsp. ground ancho chile pepper
- ½ tsp. ground coriander
- ⅛ tsp. ground cumin
  Dash cayenne pepper

1. Remove and discard thick stems from kale. Coarsely chop leaves (should have about 8 cups). In a large bowl combine chopped kale and next five ingredients (through pumpkin seeds).
2. For vinaigrette, remove ½ tsp. zest and squeeze ¼ cup juice from limes. In a small bowl whisk together lime zest and juice and the remaining ingredients. Drizzle kale mixture with vinaigrette; toss to coat.

Tip Tuscan kale has many different names: cavolo nero, black cabbage, lacinato, and dinosaur to name a few. It has a better texture for raw preparations than the curly leaf variety.

PER SERVING (about 2 cups each) **CAL** 199, **FAT** 11 g (2 g sat. fat), **CHOL** 4 mg, **SODIUM** 309 mg, **CARB** 22 g (3 g fiber, 9 g sugars), **PRO** 7 g

Grilled Portobello-
Chicken Row Salad

Grilled Portobello-Chicken Row Salad

18 g
CARB

SERVES 4
TOTAL 45 min.

- 1 teaspoon fennel seeds, finely crushed
- 1 teaspoon dried Italian seasoning, crushed
- ⅛ to ¼ tsp. crushed red pepper
- 12 oz. skinless, boneless chicken breast halves
- 4 large fresh portobello mushrooms, stemmed
- 1 medium red sweet pepper, halved and seeded
- 1 small red onion, cut into 1-inch slices
- 3 cups torn kale
- 3 cups torn romaine lettuce
- ½ cup shredded reduced-fat Italian cheese blend (2 oz.)
- ½ cup torn fresh basil
- ½ cup light balsamic vinaigrette dressing
- 2 Tbsp. chopped walnuts, toasted

1. In a bowl combine fennel seeds, Italian seasoning, and crushed red pepper. Sprinkle over chicken.
2. Grill chicken, mushrooms, sweet pepper, and onion, covered, over medium until chicken is done (165°F) and vegetables are tender (8 to 12 minutes for vegetables and 15 to 18 minutes for chicken). Cut chicken, mushrooms, and pepper into bite-size strips. Coarsely chop onion.
3. On a platter arrange rows of chicken, vegetables, greens, cheese, and basil. Drizzle with dressing and sprinkle with walnuts.

Tip To finely crush fennel seeds, use a spice grinder or clean coffee grinder.

PER SERVING (2½ cups salad + 2 Tbsp. dressing each) **CAL** 266, **FAT** 9 g (2 g sat. fat), **CHOL** 70 mg, **SODIUM** 392 mg, **CARB** 18 g (5 g fiber, 10 g sugars), **PRO** 29 g

Arugula Chicken Paillard

20 g **CARB** | **SERVES** 4
TOTAL 20 min.

4 small skinless, boneless chicken breast halves (about 1¼ lb. total)
Olive oil
3 cups arugula
2 cups shredded fresh baby spinach
2 pink grapefruit, peeled and sliced
1 medium avocado, halved, seeded, peeled, and sliced
¾ cup thinly sliced fennel
1 recipe Champagne Vinaigrette

1. Using the flat side of a meat mallet, flatten chicken between two pieces of plastic wrap to ¼ to ½ inch thick.

2. Lightly grease a panini griddle, covered indoor electric grill, or large skillet with olive oil. Heat over medium or according to manufacturer's directions. Add chicken. If using griddle or grill, close lid and cook about 4 minutes or until no longer pink (165°F). (If using skillet, cook about 8 minutes, turning once.)
3. Arrange chicken and next five ingredients (through fennel) on plates. Drizzle with Champagne Vinaigrette.

Champagne Vinaigrette In a bowl whisk together **2 Tbsp. grapefruit juice, 1 Tbsp. each champagne vinegar and olive oil,** and **¼ tsp. each salt and black pepper.**

PER SERVING (1 chicken breast half + 1¼ cups greens + ½ grapefruit + ¼ avocado + 3 Tbsp. fennel + 1 Tbsp. vinaigrette each) **CAL** 314, **FAT** 11 g (2 g sat. fat), **CHOL** 82 mg, **SODIUM** 271 mg, **CARB** 20 g (6 g fiber, 10 g sugars), **PRO** 35 g

Arugula Chicken Paillard

Asian Beef
Cabbage Salad

Asian Beef and Cabbage Salad

17g CARB | **SERVES** 6
TOTAL 35 min.

4 cups packaged shredded broccoli slaw mix
3 cups packaged shredded cabbage with carrot (coleslaw mix)
3 medium red sweet peppers, cut into bite-size strips
¾ cup bias-sliced snow pea pods
½ cup thinly sliced red onion
½ cup light mayonnaise
⅓ cup light Asian salad dressing
3 Tbsp. rice vinegar
2 Tbsp. lime juice
2 Tbsp. reduced-sodium soy sauce
Nonstick cooking spray
1 pound lean ground beef (95% lean)
½ cup sliced green onions
¼ cup fresh cilantro leaves
1 fresh jalapeño chile pepper, seeded (if desired) and sliced (tip, p. 154) (optional)

1. In a large bowl combine the first five ingredients (through red onion). Add mayonnaise and Asian dressing; stir to coat.
2. In a small bowl combine the next three ingredients (through soy sauce).
3. Coat a 10-inch nonstick skillet with cooking spray; heat skillet over medium. Add ground beef; cook until browned. Drain off fat. Stir in soy sauce mixture; cook until liquid is nearly evaporated. Remove from heat. Stir in green onions.
4. Spoon meat mixture over slaw mixture. Top with cilantro and, if desired, jalepeño pepper.

PER SERVING *(1⅔ cups each)* **CAL** 239, **FAT** 10 g (3 g sat. fat), **CHOL** 50 mg, **SODIUM** 555 mg, **CARB** 17 g (3 g fiber, 9 g sugars), **PRO** 19 g

**Hot Gingered Beef
and Broccoli Salad**

Hot Gingered Beef and Broccoli Salad

14 g
CARB

SERVES 4
TOTAL 20 min.

- 12 oz. boneless beef sirloin steak, trimmed of fat
- ½ cup light ginger vinaigrette salad dressing
- 3 cups broccoli florets
- 8 cups mixed spring salad greens or baby salad greens
- 1 medium red sweet pepper, seeded and cut into bite-size strips

1. Thinly slice meat across the grain into bite-size strips.
2. In a 10-inch skillet or wok heat 2 Tbsp. of the dressing over medium-high. Add broccoli; cook and stir 3 minutes. Add meat; cook and stir 2 to 3 minutes more or until meat is slightly pink in center.
3. Transfer meat mixture to a large bowl; add greens and sweet pepper. Drizzle with the remaining dressing; toss gently to coat.

PER SERVING (2½ cups each) **CAL** 194, **FAT** 6 g (1 g sat. fat), **CHOL** 51 mg, **SODIUM** 475 mg, **CARB** 14 g (4 g fiber, 7 g sugars), **PRO** 22 g

Blackberry Salad with Pork

Blackberry Salad with Pork

28 g
CARB

SERVES 4
HANDS ON 25 min.
TOTAL 50 min.

- 1 10- to 12-oz. pork tenderloin
- ¼ tsp. salt
- ¼ tsp. black pepper
- 2½ cups blackberries and/or raspberries
- ¼ cup lemon juice
- 1½ Tbsp. olive oil
- 3 Tbsp. honey
- 6 cups packaged mixed baby salad greens (spring mix)
- 2 cups blackberries and/or raspberries
- 1 cup grape tomatoes, halved
- 2 Tbsp. pine nuts, toasted (optional)

1. Preheat oven to 425°F. Place pork on a rack in a shallow roasting pan. Sprinkle with ⅛ tsp each of the salt and pepper. Roast, uncovered, about 20 minutes or until a thermometer registers 145°F. Remove from oven. Cover roast with foil and let stand 3 minutes. Cool slightly. Cut pork into ¼-inch-thick slices.
2. For blackberry dressing, in a small food processor or blender combine ½ cup of the blackberries, the lemon juice, oil, honey, and the remaining ¼ tsp. each salt and pepper. Cover and process or blend until smooth. Strain dressing through a fine-mesh sieve; discard seeds.

3. Divide greens among salad bowls or plates. Top with the remaining 2 cups blackberries, the tomatoes, pine nuts (if using), and pork slices. Drizzle with dressing. Serve immediately.

Tip To toast pine nuts, place them in a shallow baking pan lined with parchment paper. Bake in a 350°F oven 5 to 7 minutes, shaking pan once or twice. Watch closely so nuts don't burn.

PER SERVING (1½ cups greens + 2 oz. cooked pork + ½ cup berries + 2 Tbsp. dressing each) **CAL** 283, **FAT** 13 g (2 g sat. fat), **CHOL** 46 mg, **SODIUM** 147 mg, **CARB** 28 g (7 g fiber, 20 g sugars), **PRO** 18 g

QUICK TIP Use a mixture of tender spring greens instead of plain spinach when they're in season.

Maple-Pork Wilted Salad

Maple-Pork Wilted Salad

23g CARB

SERVES 4
TOTAL 30 min.

- 8 cups fresh baby spinach or torn fresh spinach
- 1½ cups thinly sliced cucumber
- ⅓ cup thin wedges red onion
- 12 oz. pork tenderloin, trimmed and sliced ¼ inch thick
- ½ tsp. salt
- ½ tsp. black pepper
- 2 Tbsp. olive oil
- 2 Tbsp. finely chopped shallot
- ¼ cup cider vinegar
- ¼ cup pure maple syrup
- ¼ cup sliced almonds, toasted

1. In a large bowl combine spinach, cucumber, and onion. Sprinkle meat with ¼ tsp. each of the salt and pepper.
2. In a 10-inch skillet heat 1 Tbsp. of the oil over medium-high. Add meat; cook 2 to 3 minutes or just until slightly pink in center, turning once. Add meat to spinach mixture.
3. For dressing, in skillet heat remaining 1 Tbsp. oil over medium. Add shallot; cook and stir about 2 minutes or until tender. Stir in vinegar and maple syrup. Simmer, uncovered, 1½ to 2 minutes or until slightly thickened. Season with the remaining ¼ tsp. each salt and pepper.
4. Pour dressing over spinach mixture; toss gently to coat. Top with almonds.

PER SERVING *(2 cups each)* **CAL** 325, **FAT** 15 g (4 g sat. fat), **CHOL** 67 mg, **SODIUM** 349 mg, **CARB** 23 g (3 g fiber, 0 g sugars), **PRO** 24 g

Potato and Brussels Sprouts Salad with Lemon-Honey Vinaigrette

34g CARB

SERVES 6
TOTAL 40 min.

- 12 oz. medium red potatoes, quartered
- 1 recipe Lemon-Honey Vinaigrette
- 6 slices lower-sodium, less-fat bacon, chopped
- 2 cups fresh Brussels sprouts, trimmed and quartered
- ½ cup halved and thinly sliced red onion
- 3 Tbsp. water
- 1 cup chopped tomatoes
- 1 15-oz. can no-salt-added garbanzo beans (chickpeas), rinsed and drained
- 6 cups torn butterhead lettuce
- ½ cup crumbled reduced-fat feta cheese (2 oz.)

1. In a covered medium saucepan cook potatoes in enough boiling water to cover 12 to 15 minutes or until tender; drain.
2. Meanwhile, prepare Lemon-Honey Vinaigrette. In a 10-inch skillet cook bacon over medium until crisp, stirring occasionally. Drain bacon on paper towels; discard drippings.
3. Add Brussels sprouts, onion, and the water to skillet. Cook, covered, over medium 4 to 6 minutes or until sprouts are crisp-tender, stirring occasionally. Add tomatoes. Cook, uncovered, 2 to 3 minutes or until tomatoes are softened and sprouts are lightly browned, stirring occasionally. Remove from heat. Stir in potatoes and beans.
4. Divide lettuce among plates. Top with potato mixture and drizzle with vinaigrette. Sprinkle with cheese and the reserved bacon.

Lemon-Honey Vinaigrette In a screw-top jar combine ⅓ **cup lemon juice, 2 Tbsp. each olive oil and honey, 2 tsp. Dijon-style mustard, and ⅛ tsp. salt.** Cover and shake well.

PER SERVING *(2 cups each)* **CAL** 246, **FAT** 8 g (2 g sat. fat), **CHOL** 7 mg, **SODIUM** 351 mg, **CARB** 34 g (6 g fiber, 10 g sugars), **PRO** 11 g

Potato and Brussels Sprouts Salad with Lemon-Honey Vinaigrette

BLT Salad with
Buttermilk Dressing

BLT Salad with Buttermilk Dressing

12 g
CARB

SERVES 4
TOTAL 30 min.

2 Tbsp. light sour cream or crème fraîche
2 Tbsp. light mayonnaise
1 Tbsp. snipped fresh dill weed
1 Tbsp. apple cider vinegar
1 clove garlic, minced
¼ cup buttermilk or sour milk
¼ tsp. salt
¼ tsp. freshly ground black pepper
2 heads romaine lettuce
   Olive oil
4 slices lower-sodium, less-fat bacon, crisp-cooked
1 cup cherry tomatoes, halved
½ cup finely shredded Parmesan cheese (2 oz.)

1. For dressing, in a bowl whisk together the first five ingredients (through garlic). Whisk in buttermilk and ⅛ tsp. each salt and pepper.
2. Cut each head of lettuce in half lengthwise. Brush the lettuce halves all over with oil; sprinkle with the remaining ⅛ tsp. each salt and pepper. Grill lettuce, uncovered, over medium about 2 minutes or until lightly charred, turning once.
3. Place lettuce portions on a platter with bacon and cherry tomatoes. Drizzle lettuce with dressing and top with cheese.

Tip To make ¼ cup sour milk, place 1 tsp. lemon juice or vinegar in a glass measuring cup. Add enough milk to make ¼ cup total liquid; stir. Let stand 5 minutes before using.

PER SERVING (½ romaine head + 1 slice bacon + ¼ cup tomatoes + 2 Tbsp. Parmesan + 1½ Tbsp. dressing each) **CAL** 208, **FAT** 14 g (4 g sat. fat), **CHOL** 15 mg, **SODIUM** 489 mg, **CARB** 12 g (6 g fiber, 5 g sugars), **PRO** 10 g

Lemony Tuna Salad

7 g
CARB

SERVES 4
TOTAL 20 min.

1 lemon
½ cup chopped fennel bulb
½ cup thinly sliced red onion
1 5-oz. pkg. arugula or mixed spring greens
2 5-oz. cans tuna, drained and broken into chunks
1 cup cherry tomatoes, halved
¼ tsp. salt
¼ tsp. black pepper

1. Remove 1 tsp. zest and squeeze 3 Tbsp. juice from lemon.
2. In a large bowl combine lemon zest and juice, fennel, and onion. Add arugula, tuna, tomatoes, salt, and pepper; toss gently to coat.

PER SERVING (1½ cups each) **CAL** 104, **FAT** 2 g (1 g sat. fat), **CHOL** 24 mg, **SODIUM** 377 mg, **CARB** 7 g (2 g fiber, 3 g sugars), **PRO** 15 g

Seared Sesame Tuna
with Fennel-Apple Slaw

Shrimp and Quinoa Salad

42 g CARB

SERVES 4
HANDS ON 30 min.
TOTAL 45 min.

- 10 oz. fresh or frozen large shrimp
- 1 cup quinoa
- 2 Cara Cara and/or navel oranges
- 3 Tbsp. white balsamic vinegar
- ¼ tsp. salt
- ¼ tsp. black pepper
- 1 5- to 6-oz. pkg. baby spinach or arugula

1. Thaw shrimp, if frozen. If using wooden skewers, soak them in enough water to cover at least 30 minutes before using. Peel and devein shrimp, leaving tails intact if desired. Rinse shrimp; pat dry. Thread shrimp on four 8-inch skewers. Grill skewers, covered, over medium 4 to 6 minutes or until shrimp are opaque, turning once.
2. Meanwhile, rinse quinoa; drain. In a medium saucepan bring 2 cups *water* to boiling. Add quinoa. Return to boiling; reduce heat. Simmer, covered, about 15 minutes or until water is absorbed. Remove from heat.
3. Remove 1 tsp. zest from one of the oranges. Using a paring knife, cut remaining peel and white pith from oranges; discard. Holding an orange over an extra-large bowl to catch juices, cut segments from orange (set segments aside). Squeeze juice from membranes into bowl. Repeat with remaining orange. Stir in orange zest, balsamic vinegar, salt, and pepper. Add shrimp, quinoa, and spinach; toss gently to combine. Arrange orange segments over shrimp mixture.

PER SERVING *(2 cups each)* **CAL** 271, **FAT** 3 g (0 g sat. fat), **CHOL** 99 mg, **SODIUM** 248 mg, **CARB** 42 g (5 g fiber, 11 g sugars), **PRO** 20 g

Seared Sesame Tuna with Fennel-Apple Slaw

16 g CARB

SERVES 4
TOTAL 30 min.

- 2 5- to 6-oz. fresh or frozen tuna steaks, cut ¾ inch thick
- 1 recipe Fennel-Apple Slaw
- ¼ tsp. salt
- ¼ tsp. black pepper
- 2 egg whites
- 1 Tbsp. water
- ¼ cup panko bread crumbs
- 2 Tbsp. sesame seeds
- 1 Tbsp. canola oil
- 4 cups fresh spinach

1. Thaw tuna, if frozen. Prepare Fennel-Apple Slaw. Rinse tuna; pat dry. Sprinkle with salt and pepper.
2. In a shallow dish combine egg whites and the water. In another shallow dish combine bread crumbs and sesame seeds. Dip tuna in egg white mixture, then in crumb mixture to coat; press lightly.

3. In a 10-inch nonstick skillet heat oil over medium-high. Add tuna; cook 5 to 7 minutes or just until tuna flakes, turning once (tuna will be pink in center). Cut into ¼-inch slices.
4. Divide spinach among plates and top with slaw and tuna. If desired, sprinkle with the reserved fronds.

Fennel-Apple Slaw Trim and core ½ of a medium fennel bulb, reserving feathery tops (if desired). Thinly slice fennel. In a bowl combine fennel; **1 cup thin, bite-size strips green apple;** ½ cup coarsely shredded carrot; and ⅓ cup halved and very thinly sliced radishes. In a bowl whisk together 3 Tbsp. rice vinegar; 2 Tbsp. snipped fresh mint; 4 tsp. canola oil; ¼ tsp. each salt and, if desired, toasted sesame oil; and ⅛ to ¼ tsp. crushed red pepper. Add to fennel mixture; toss.

PER SERVING *(2¼ oz. tuna + ¾ cup slaw, + 1 cup spinach each)* **CAL** 251, **FAT** 10 g (1 g sat. fat), **CHOL** 28 mg, **SODIUM** 435 mg, **CARB** 16 g (5 g fiber, 6 g sugars), **PRO** 22 g

Shrimp and Quinoa Salad

⌃⌃ **QUICK TIP** To use a grill pan, lightly brush grill pan with olive oil. Heat pan over medium-high. Add skewers; cook 4 to 6 minutes or until shrimp are opaque, turning once.

Quick Scallop
and Noodle Salad

Quick Scallop and Noodle Salad

9g CARB | **SERVES** 4
| **TOTAL** 30 min.

- 12 fresh or frozen sea scallops (about 18 oz. total)
- 1 medium zucchini, trimmed
- ½ tsp. olive oil
- 2 Tbsp. orange juice
- 2 Tbsp. champagne or cider vinegar
- 1 Tbsp. toasted sesame oil
- 1 tsp. grated fresh ginger
- ½ tsp. lime zest
- ½ tsp. salt
- 1½ cups torn fresh spinach
- 1 cup chopped cucumber
- ⅔ cup thinly sliced radishes
- ¼ tsp. black pepper
- 1 Tbsp. olive oil
- 2 Tbsp. sesame seeds, toasted

1. Thaw scallops, if frozen. Using a vegetable spiralizer, julienne cutter, or mandoline, cut zucchini into long, thin noodles. In a 10-inch skillet heat the ½ tsp. olive oil over medium-high. Add zucchini noodles. Cook and stir about 1 minute or just until tender; cool.
2. Meanwhile, in a large bowl combine next five ingredients (through lime zest) and ¼ tsp. of the salt. Stir in noodles, spinach, cucumber, and radishes.
3. Rinse scallops; pat dry. Sprinkle with remaining ¼ tsp. salt and the pepper.
4. In same skillet heat the 1 Tbsp. olive oil over medium-high. Add scallops; cook 3 to 5 minutes or until opaque, turning once. Serve noodle mixture with scallops; sprinkle with sesame seeds.

Tip To toast sesame seeds, spread seeds in a dry skillet. Cook over medium heat until light brown, stirring frequently so they don't burn.

PER SERVING (3 scallops + 1¼ cups noodle mixture each) **CAL** 227, **FAT** 10 g (1 g sat. fat), **CHOL** 42 mg, **SODIUM** 527 mg, **CARB** 9 g (2 g fiber, 3 g sugars), **PRO** 24 g

Spicy Black Bean and Romaine Salad with Garlic-Lime Crema

34g CARB | **SERVES** 4
| **TOTAL** 30 min.

- 1 lime
- ¼ cup finely chopped red onion
- 1 15-oz. can reduced-sodium black beans, rinsed and drained
- 1 medium poblano chile, seeded and cut into thin bite-size strips (tip, p. 154)
- 1 cup cherry tomatoes, quartered
- ½ cup frozen yellow sweet corn kernels, thawed
- ⅓ cup light sour cream
- 1 Tbsp. canola oil
- ½ tsp. minced garlic
- ⅛ tsp. salt
- 4 cups torn fresh romaine lettuce
- 1 medium avocado, halved, seeded, peeled, and chopped
- ½ cup crumbled Cotija cheese or reduced-fat feta cheese (2 oz.)

1. Remove ½ tsp. zest and squeeze 3 Tbsp. juice from lime. In a small bowl combine red onion and lime juice. Press down on onion to submerge it as much as possible in juice. In a medium bowl combine black beans, poblano chile, tomatoes, and corn.
2. Spoon 2 Tbsp. of the lime juice from the onion into a small bowl. Add sour cream, canola oil, garlic, salt, and lime zest. Whisk until smooth. Arrange lettuce on plates. Drizzle with sour cream dressing. Top with bean mixture, avocado, red onion, and cheese.

Tip For a higher-protein meal, add 1 lb. cooked peeled and deveined shrimp.

PER SERVING (2 cups each) **CAL** 303, **FAT** 15 g (5 g sat. fat), **CHOL** 20 mg, **SODIUM** 476 mg, **CARB** 34 g (9 g fiber, 4 g sugars), **PRO** 12 g

Spicy Black Bean and Romaine Salad with Garlic-Lime Crema

Wild Rice and Bean Salad with Peaches and Feta

35 g CARB

SERVES 2
HANDS ON 15 min.
TOTAL 1 hr. 55 min.

- 1½ cups low-sodium vegetable broth
- ½ cup uncooked wild rice, rinsed and drained
- 2 Tbsp. lime juice
- 1 Tbsp. olive oil
- 1 tsp. snipped fresh mint
- ¼ tsp. salt
- 2 cups baby arugula
- 1 medium peach, peeled (if desired) and sliced
- ½ cup canned no-salt-added cannellini (white kidney) beans, rinsed and drained
- ¼ cup crumbled reduced-fat feta cheese (1 oz.)
  Black pepper (optional)
  Lime wedges (optional)

1. In a large saucepan bring broth to boiling. Stir in rice; reduce heat. Simmer, covered, about 40 minutes or until rice is tender. Drain and cool. In a medium bowl combine the next four ingredients (through salt). Stir in half of the wild rice (reserve remaining rice for another use). Cover and chill 1 to 24 hours.

2. Add the next four ingredients (through cheese) to rice mixture; toss gently to combine. If desired, sprinkle with pepper and additional mint and serve with lime wedges.

PER SERVING *(2¼ cups each)* **CAL** 261, **FAT** 11 g (3 g sat. fat), **CHOL** 10 mg, **SODIUM** 534 mg, **CARB** 35 g (6 g fiber, 8 g sugars), **PRO** 10 g

Wild Rice and Bean Salad
with Peaches and Feta

3

COMFORTING
SOUPS & STEWS

Soup checks all the boxes for an easy, complete, feel-good meal.

Whether it's a long-simmering slow cooker stew or a simple

heat-and-eat bowl, soup is satisfyingly delicious. Try everything

from zesty Kickin' Hot Chili, robust Hearty Chicken Stew, cool

and refreshing Summer Fresh Gazpacho, to silky-smooth

Cauliflower Soup.

Chicken and Zucchini Stew with Olive Gremolata

15 g
CARB

SERVES 8
HANDS ON 30 min.
SLOW COOK 5 hr. 15 min.

- ¾ cup chopped red sweet pepper
- ½ cup chopped onion
- ½ cup chopped carrot
- ½ oz. dried porcini or shiitake mushrooms
- ¼ tsp. salt
- ¼ tsp. black pepper
- 6 bone-in chicken thighs (2¼ lb. total), skinned
- 2 14.5-oz. cans no-salt-added diced tomatoes
- 2 cups reduced-sodium chicken broth
- 3½ cups sliced halved zucchini
- 2 Tbsp. balsamic vinegar
- ⅓ cup pimiento-stuffed green olives, chopped
- 2 Tbsp. coarsely snipped fresh basil
- 1 Tbsp. orange or lemon zest
- 1 Tbsp. snipped fresh rosemary or 1 tsp. dried rosemary, crushed

1. In a 4- to 5-qt. slow cooker combine the first six ingredients (through pepper). Lay chicken on vegetables, overlapping as needed. Top with diced tomatoes and broth.
2. Cover and cook on low 5 to 6 hours or on high 2½ to 3 hours.
3. Using a slotted spoon, transfer chicken to a large bowl. When chicken is cool enough to handle, remove meat from bones; discard bones. Shred chicken using two forks. Return chicken to slow cooker; add zucchini and vinegar. If slow cooker is on low, turn to high. Cover and cook about 15 minutes more or until zucchini is just tender.
4. Meanwhile, in a bowl combine the remaining ingredients. Top servings of stew with olive mixture.

PER SERVING (1½ cups each) **CAL** 206, **FAT** 6 g (1 g sat. fat), **CHOL** 97 mg, **SODIUM** 555 mg, **CARB** 15 g (5 g fiber, 10 g sugars), **PRO** 24 g

Chicken and Zucchini Stew with Olive Gremolata

Hearty Chicken Stew

24 g
CARB

SERVES 4
HANDS ON 25 min.
TOTAL 45 min.

- 2 tsp. canola oil
- 4 skinless, boneless chicken thighs, cut into 1½-inch pieces (about 1 lb. total)
- 2 cups thinly sliced carrots
- 1 cup thinly sliced celery
- ⅔ cup thinly sliced leek
- 3 cloves garlic, minced
- 2 cups reduced-sodium chicken broth
- ¾ cup cubed red potato
- 1 cup frozen cut green beans
- 2 tsp. snipped fresh rosemary or 1 tsp. dried rosemary, crushed
- ¼ tsp. black pepper
- ½ cup fat-free milk
- 1 Tbsp. all-purpose flour
  Cracked black pepper

1. In a 4-qt. Dutch oven heat oil over medium. Add the next five ingredients (through garlic). Cook and stir 5 to 8 minutes or until chicken is browned on all sides and vegetables are starting to soften. Stir in the next five ingredients (through ¼ tsp. black pepper). Bring to boiling; reduce heat. Simmer, covered, 20 to 25 minutes or until vegetables are tender and chicken is no longer pink.
2. Meanwhile, in a bowl whisk together milk and flour until smooth. Stir into cooked stew. Return to boiling; reduce heat. Cook and stir about 2 minutes or until stew is thickened. Sprinkle servings with cracked black pepper.

PER SERVING (1¾ cups each) **CAL** 269, **FAT** 7 g (1 g sat. fat), **CHOL** 108 mg, **SODIUM** 462 mg, **CARB** 24 g (4 g fiber, 8 g sugars), **PRO** 27 g

QUICK TIP Change it up by substituting frozen peas and/or corn for the green beans.

Hearty Chicken Stew

Turkey Soup in a Jar

29 g
CARB

SERVES 1
TOTAL 20 min.

- 1 tsp. reduced-sodium chicken base
- 1 clove garlic, minced
- ½ tsp. lemon zest
  Pinch ground ginger
- 2 Tbsp. dried whole wheat couscous
- ⅔ cup shredded or chopped cooked turkey breast or chicken breast
- 2 Tbsp. sliced green onion
- ¼ cup thinly sliced red sweet pepper
- 3 fresh shiitake mushrooms, stemmed and thinly sliced
- ½ cup packed fresh baby spinach

1. In a microwavable pint-size jar with lid layer all ingredients in the order given. Place lid on jar. Store in the refrigerator up to 3 days.

2. Before heating, let stand at room temperature 10 minutes or run warm water over the jar for a minute or so to warm slightly. Fill the jar nearly full with water (about 1 cup). Microwave, uncovered, 2 minutes. Cover; let stand 5 minutes. Stir to combine. (Or fill the jar with hot water from a desktop kettle or hot water dispenser. Cover and let stand 5 minutes. Stir to combine.)

To Tote Pack jar in an insulated bag with ice packs.

PER SERVING *(2 cups)* **CAL** 254, **FAT** 3 g (1 g sat. fat), **CHOL** 60 mg, **SODIUM** 617 mg, **CARB** 29 g (6 g fiber, 4 g sugars), **PRO** 32 g

Beef Posole

Beef Posole

24 g CARB

SERVES 6
HANDS ON 25 min.
SLOW COOK 7 hr. 30 min.

- 8 oz. round red potatoes, chopped
- 1 large onion, cut into thin wedges
- 1 lb. beef flank steak, cut into 6 pieces
- 2 14.5-oz. cans 50%-less-sodium beef broth
- 1 15.5-oz. can golden or white hominy, rinsed and drained
- 1 14.5-oz. can diced tomatoes
- 1 fresh poblano chile pepper, chopped (tip, p. 154)
- 1 Tbsp. hot chili powder
- 3 cloves garlic, minced
- ½ tsp. ground cumin
- ¼ tsp. salt
- 3 cups shredded cabbage
  Chopped fresh cilantro
  Lime wedges
  Crumbled queso fresco (optional)
  Sliced hot chile peppers (optional) (tip, p. 154)

1. In a 4- to 5-qt. slow cooker place potatoes and onion. Top with flank steak. In a bowl combine the next eight ingredients (through salt). Pour over meat. Cover and cook on low 7 hours or on high 3½ hours.

2. If slow cooker is on low, turn to high. Add cabbage. Cover and cook 30 to 60 minutes or until cabbage is tender. Transfer meat to a cutting board. Shred meat using two forks; return to slow cooker. Sprinkle servings with cilantro and, if desired, queso fresco and sliced chile peppers. Serve with lime wedges.

PER SERVING (1⅔ cups each) **CAL** 231, **FAT** 6 g (2 g sat. fat), **CHOL** 49 mg, **SODIUM** 755 mg, **CARB** 24 g (5 g fiber, 6 g sugars), **PRO** 20 g

Kickin' Hot Chili

Potato-Leek and Ham Soup with Swiss Cheese Toasts

26 g
CARB

SERVES 6
TOTAL 30 min.

1 cup thinly sliced leeks
1 Tbsp. canola oil
3 cloves garlic, minced
3 cups reduced-sodium chicken broth
1½ cups water
1 15-oz. can no-salt-added navy beans or Great Northern beans, rinsed and drained
1 medium Yukon gold potato (5 to 6 oz.), cut into ½-inch cubes
1 cup frozen cut green beans
1 medium red sweet pepper, cut into thin bite-size strips (¾ cup)
6 oz. lower-sodium cooked ham, cubed
6 ½-inch-thick diagonal slices whole grain baguette-style bread
¾ cup shredded Swiss cheese (3 oz.)

1. In a 4-qt. Dutch oven cook leeks in hot oil over medium-low 5 minutes, stirring occasionally. Stir in garlic.
2. Add the next seven ingredient (through ham). Bring to boiling; reduce heat. Simmer, covered, 10 to 12 minutes or until potato and green beans are tender.
3. Meanwhile, preheat broiler. Line a small baking sheet with foil. Place bread slices on prepared baking sheet. Broil 4 inches from the heat about 1 minute or until toasted. Turn slices and top evenly with cheese. Broil about 1 minute more or until cheese is melted and just starting to bubble and brown. Serve toasts with soup.

PER SERVING *(1¼ cups soup + 1 toast each)* **CAL** 251, **FAT** 9 g (4 g sat. fat), **CHOL** 27 mg, **SODIUM** 587 mg, **CARB** 26 g (6 g fiber, 3 g sugars), **PRO** 17 g

Kickin' Hot Chili

25 g
CARB

SERVES 8
HANDS ON 25 min.
SLOW COOK 8 hr.

1½ lb. lean ground beef
2 cups chopped onions
1 15-oz. can dark red kidney beans, rinsed and drained
½ cup chopped green or red sweet pepper
3½ cups water
2 6-oz. can no-salt-added tomato paste
1 14.5-oz. can no-salt-added diced tomatoes, undrained
1 4-oz. can diced green chile peppers, undrained
1 Tbsp. minced garlic
1 Tbsp. yellow mustard

1 tsp. chili powder
1 tsp. black pepper
½ tsp. ground cumin
¼ tsp. salt
¼ tsp. cayenne pepper

1. In 10-inch skillet cook ground beef and onion over medium until meat is browned. Drain off fat.
2. In 4- to 5-qt. slow cooker combine ground beef mixture, beans, and chopped sweet pepper. Add the remaining ingredients.
3. Cover and cook on low 8 to 10 hours or on high 4 to 5 hours. If desired, top servings with *green and/or red pepper strips*.

PER SERVING *(1¼ cups each)* **CAL** 253, **FAT** 9 g (3 g sat. fat), **CHOL** 54 mg, **SODIUM** 320 mg, **CARB** 25 g (7 g fiber, 8 g sugars), **PRO** 22 g

QUICK TIP For a thicker soup, slightly mash the potatoes and beans at the end of Step 2.

**Potato-Leek and Ham Soup
with Swiss Cheese Toasts**

Asian Pork and Veggie Noodle Bowls

15 g CARB

SERVES 4
TOTAL 35 min.

Nonstick cooking spray
12 oz. pork tenderloin, cut into very thin bite-size strips
½ cup water
2 Tbsp. white miso paste or reduced-sodium soy sauce
2 cups thinly sliced, stemmed shiitake mushrooms or thinly sliced button mushrooms
½ cup thinly sliced shallot
2 tsp. toasted sesame oil
2 Tbsp. finely chopped fresh ginger
2 14.5-oz. cans reduced-sodium chicken broth
2 medium carrots, peeled
1 cup snow peas or sugar snap peas, bias-cut into 1-inch pieces
1 medium yellow summer squash or zucchini
2 radishes, thinly sliced
1 tsp. sesame seeds, toasted

1. Coat a 4- to 6-qt. nonstick Dutch oven with cooking spray. Heat over medium-high. Add pork strips. Cook 2 minutes. Remove pork from pan.
2. In a bowl whisk together water and miso paste. In the same Dutch oven cook mushrooms and shallot in hot sesame oil over medium 5 minutes, stirring occasionally. Add ginger; cook and stir 30 seconds. Add miso mixture and broth to the mushroom mixture. Bring to boiling.
3. Meanwhile, using a vegetable peeler, cut ribbons from carrot. Use a spiralizer or julienne peeler to make long thin noodles with the summer squash or zucchini. Add carrot strips and peas to mushroom mixture. Cook, uncovered, 3 minutes. Add reserved pork and the squash noodles; cook about 30 seconds or just until heated.
4. Top servings with radish slices and sesame seeds.

Asian Pork and Veggie Noodle Bowls

Tip Partially freeze pork for easier slicing.

Tip If you do not have a spiralizer or julienne peeler, use a knife to cut the squash or zucchini into thin bite-size strips.

PER SERVING (2 cups each) **CAL** 197, **FAT** 5 g (1 g sat. fat), **CHOL** 55 mg, **SODIUM** 810 mg, **CARB** 15 g (4 g fiber, 7 g sugars), **PRO** 25 g

Vegetable and Pasta Soup

38 g CARB

SERVES 6
HANDS ON 20 min.
SLOW COOK 7 hr. 45 min.

- 1 15-oz. can cannellini (white kidney) beans, rinsed and drained
- 1 cup frozen whole kernel corn
- 1 cup chopped onion
- 1 cup finely chopped carrots
- 1 cup coarsely chopped zucchini
- 2 cloves garlic, minced
- 6 cups unsalted vegetable stock or unsalted chicken stock
- 1 6-oz. can no-salt-added tomato paste
- 2 tsp. dried Italian seasoning, crushed
- ½ tsp. salt
- 1 9-oz. pkg. frozen Italian green beans
- 2 oz. dried multigrain rotini or elbow pasta
- 2 Tbsp. snipped fresh parsley
- 6 to 8 tsp. finely shredded Parmesan cheese

1. In a 3½- to 5-qt. slow cooker combine the first six ingredients (through garlic). Stir in stock, tomato paste, Italian seasoning, and salt.
2. Cover and cook on low 7 to 8 hours or on high 3½ to 4 hours.
3. If slow cooker is on low, turn to high. Stir in frozen green beans and pasta. Cover and cook 45 minutes more. Before serving, stir in parsley. Sprinkle servings with cheese.

PER SERVING *(1¾ cups each)* **CAL** 202, **FAT** 1 g (0 g sat. fat), **CHOL** 1 mg, **SODIUM** 549 mg, **CARB** 38 g (9 g fiber, 10 g sugars), **PRO** 9 g

Vegetable and Pasta Soup

New England-
Style Hearty
Clam Chowder

New England-Style Hearty Clam Chowder

42 g CARB

SERVES 4
TOTAL 35 min.

- 2 Tbsp. unsalted butter
- 1 cup chopped onion
- 1 cup chopped celery
- 2 cloves garlic, minced
- ½ tsp. dried thyme, crushed
- ¼ tsp. black pepper
- ½ cup dry white wine or 2 Tbsp. lemon juice
- ¼ cup all-purpose flour
- 2 cups low-fat (1%) milk
- ½ cup unsalted vegetable stock or reduced-sodium chicken broth
- 2 cups frozen baby lima beans, thawed
- 1 10-oz. can whole baby clams, undrained
- ½ cup snipped fresh Italian parsley
- 4 slices lower-sodium, less-fat bacon, crisp-cooked and coarsely crumbled

1. In a large saucepan melt butter over medium. Add onion and celery; cook 5 minutes or until tender, stirring occasionally. Add garlic, thyme, and pepper; cook and stir 2 minutes. If using wine, remove pan from heat and carefully add to saucepan. Return to heat and cook until nearly evaporated.
2. Sprinkle with flour; cook and stir 1 minute. Stir in milk and stock. Bring just to boiling. Cook and stir until sightly thick. Stir in beans, clams, ¼ cup of the parsley, and, if using, the lemon juice; heat through.
3. Top servings with bacon and the remaining ¼ cup parsley.

PER SERVING *(1⅓ cups each)* **CAL** 378, **FAT** 10 g (5 g sat. fat), **CHOL** 76 mg, **SODIUM** 577 mg, **CARB** 42 g (7 g fiber, 9 g sugars), **PRO** 26 g

Vegetable-Pork Oven Stew

40 g CARB

SERVES 6
HANDS ON 30 min.
TOTAL 3 hr.

- 2 Tbsp. vegetable oil
- 1¾ lb. boneless pork shoulder or pork stew meat, trimmed and cut into 1-inch pieces
- 1½ cups coarsely chopped onions
- 2 14.5-oz. cans reduced-sodium chicken broth
- 1 tsp. dried thyme, crushed
- 1 tsp. dried oregano, crushed
- 1 tsp. lemon-pepper seasoning
- ½ tsp. salt
- ⅓ cup all-purpose flour
- 1 16-oz. pkg. frozen whole kernel corn, thawed
- 1 lb. tiny new potatoes, halved
- 8 oz. fresh green beans, trimmed and cut into 1½-inch pieces, or 2 cups frozen cut green beans, thawed

1. Preheat oven to 325°F. In a 12-inch skillet heat 1 Tbsp. of the oil over medium-high. Add two-thirds of the meat and cook about 5 minutes or until browned. Transfer browned meat to 3-qt. rectangular baking dish. Repeat with remaining oil and meat and the onions. Add 1 cup of the chicken broth to skillet, stirring to loosen any browned bits from bottom of skillet. Transfer mixture to the baking dish. Add the thyme, oregano, lemon-pepper seasoning, and salt. Cover and bake 1 hour.
2. In a bowl whisk together the remaining ½ cup broth and the flour; stir into stew. Add the corn, potatoes, and beans. Bake, covered, 1½ to 1¾ hours more or until meat and vegetables are tender and stew is thickened.

PER SERVING *(1⅔ cups each)* **CAL** 392, **FAT** 13 g (3 g sat. fat), **CHOL** 79 mg, **SODIUM** 490 mg, **CARB** 40 g (6 g fiber, 6 g sugars), **PRO** 31 g

Vegetable-Pork Oven Stew

Vegetarian Chili

Vegetarian Chili

42 g CARB

SERVES 6
TOTAL 40 min.

- 1 Tbsp. canola oil
- 2 medium sweet potatoes, peeled and cut into 1-inch pieces
- 1 medium red sweet pepper, seeded and cut into ½-inch pieces
- ½ cup coarsely chopped onion
- 1 fresh jalapeño chile pepper, chopped (tip, p. 154)
- 1 clove garlic, minced
- 1 Tbsp. chili powder
- 1 tsp. ground cumin
- ¼ tsp. cayenne pepper
- 3 cups vegetable broth
- 1 15-oz. can reduced-sodium black beans, rinsed and drained
- 1 14.5-oz. can no-salt-added diced tomatoes, undrained
- 1 cup frozen whole kernel corn
- ¼ cup snipped fresh cilantro
- ¼ cup lime juice
- 6 Tbsp. light sour cream

1. In a 4- to 5-qt. Dutch oven heat oil over medium-high. Add the next five ingredients (through garlic). Cook and stir 4 minutes. Stir in chili powder, cumin, and cayenne pepper; cook and stir 1 minute more.
2. Add broth, beans, tomatoes, and corn. Bring to boiling; reduce heat. Simmer, uncovered, about 15 minutes or until sweet potatoes are tender, stirring occasionally.
3. Stir in cilantro and lime juice. Top servings with sour cream.

To Make Ahead Prepare as directed through Step 3; let cool. Place soup in an airtight container; cover. Store in the refrigerator up to 2 days.

PER SERVING (1⅓ cups each) **CAL** 229, **FAT** 4 g (1 g sat. fat), **CHOL** 4 mg, **SODIUM** 639 mg, **CARB** 42 g (8 g fiber, 10 g sugars), **PRO** 7 g

Summer-Fresh Gazpacho

16 g CARB

SERVES 6
HANDS ON 45 min.
TOTAL 4 hr. 45 min.

- 4 cups peeled and chopped assorted tomatoes
- ¾ cup chopped, seeded watermelon
- ¾ cup chopped yellow, orange, and/or red sweet pepper
- ½ cup chopped sweet onion
- ½ cup chopped cucumber
- 2 cloves garlic, minced
- ¼ tsp. salt
- ⅛ tsp. black pepper
- 3 Tbsp. lime juice
- 2 Tbsp. water
- ⅔ cup chopped cucumber
- ½ cup very thinly sliced sweet onion
- ½ tsp. kosher salt or sea salt
- ½ cup white wine vinegar
- ¼ cup lime juice
- ¼ cup plain fat-free Greek yogurt
- 1 Tbsp. honey
- 3 Tbsp. snipped fresh mint

1. In a large bowl combine the first eight ingredients (through black pepper). Transfer about half of the mixture to a blender or food processor. Add the 3 Tbsp. lime juice and the water. Cover and blend or process until smooth. Return to the remaining tomato mixture in the bowl; stir until combined. Cover and chill 4 to 24 hours.
2. In a small bowl combine the next three ingredients (through kosher salt). Cover and let stand 30 minutes. Transfer to a colander; rinse with cold water and drain well. Return to small bowl. Stir in vinegar and the ¼ cup lime juice; press vegetables down into liquid. Cover and chill 4 to 24 hours, stirring once or twice.
3. Before serving, in a bowl stir together yogurt and honey. Drain cucumber mixture. Top servings of soup with cucumbers, yogurt mixture, and mint.

PER SERVING (¾ cup soup + 2 Tbsp. cucumber topping + 1 Tbsp. yogurt mixture each) **CAL** 73, **FAT** 0 g, **CHOL** 0 mg, **SODIUM** 158 mg, **CARB** 16 g (3 g fiber, 10 g sugars), **PRO** 3 g

Summer-Fresh Gazpacho

Udon Noodle Bowl

Cauliflower Soup

Udon Noodle Bowl

29 g
CARB

SERVES 2
TOTAL 30 min.

- 1 tsp. sesame oil
- ½ cup quartered fresh mushrooms
- ½ cup shredded carrot
- 1 clove garlic, minced
- 2 cups low-sodium vegetable broth
- 4 tsp. reduced-sodium soy sauce
- 1 tsp. rice vinegar
- 6 oz. extra-firm tofu, cut into 1-inch cubes
- ½ of a 7.34-oz. pkg. refrigerated cooked udon noodles (any flavor), torn (discard seasoning packet)
- ½ of a medium zucchini, halved lengthwise and cut into ½-inch pieces
- ½ cup shredded red cabbage
- 2 Tbsp. thinly bias-sliced green onion
- 2 Tbsp. fresh cilantro leaves
- 1 Tbsp. chopped roasted, salted peanuts or cashews
  Lime wedges

1. In a large saucepan heat oil over medium. Add mushrooms, carrot, and garlic; cook and stir 3 minutes. Add the broth, soy sauce, and vinegar. Bring to boiling; reduce heat. Simmer, uncovered, 5 minutes, stirring occasionally. Stir in tofu, noodles, and zucchini. Return to boiling; reduce heat. Simmer, uncovered, 3 minutes more, stirring occasionally.
2. Top servings with cabbage, green onion, cilantro, and peanuts. Serve with lime wedges.

PER SERVING (2 cups each) **CAL** 257, **FAT** 10 g (1 g sat. fat), **CHOL** 0 mg, **SODIUM** 589 mg, **CARB** 29 g (4 g fiber, 8 g sugars), **PRO** 14 g

Cauliflower Soup

15 g
CARB

SERVES 1
TOTAL 20 min.

- 2 cups cooked cauliflower florets
- ⅔ to ¾ cup reduced-sodium chicken broth
  Dash garlic powder
  Dash black pepper
- 1 oz. reduced-fat cream cheese (neufchatel)
- ⅓ cup plain fat-free Greek yogurt
- 2 slices lower-sodium, less-fat bacon, crisp-cooked and crumbled
- 1 tsp. snipped fresh parsley
- ¼ tsp. lemon zest

1. In a blender or food processor combine cauliflower, ⅔ cup of the broth, the garlic powder, and pepper.

Cover and blend until smooth. If desired, cover and chill overnight.
2. Transfer cauliflower mixture to a small saucepan. Bring just to boiling over medium. Whisk in cream cheese and enough of the remaining broth to reach desired consistency; heat through. Top servings with yogurt, bacon, parsley, and lemon zest.

To Tote Transfer soup to a preheated 1-pt. insulated bottle. Place yogurt in a covered container. Place bacon, parsley, and lemon zest in another covered container. Pack insulated bottle and containers in an insulated bag. To serve, top soup with yogurt and bacon mixture.

PER SERVING (1⅓ cups) **CAL** 229, **FAT** 10 g (5 g sat. fat), **CHOL** 28 mg, **SODIUM** 348 mg, **CARB** 15 g (6 g fiber, 9 g sugars), **PRO** 21 g

4

SMART
SANDWICHES

Sandwiches can still be on the menu when you make mindful picks

for carb-smart breads and portion sizes. You'll find individual

options for something quick at home or to pack for a satisfying

lunch at work. Serve a crowd with slow-simmered beef tacos and

pulled pork sandwiches with a twist.

QUICK TIP ⌄

This sandwich is a great use for leftover roasted chicken. Or plan ahead when grilling and add extra chicken to the grill.

Chicken Club Sandwiches

Chicken Club Sandwiches

29 g
CARB

SERVES 4
TOTAL 20 min.

- ½ of an avocado, seeded and peeled
- 2 Tbsp. honey mustard
- 4 Hawaiian sweet rolls, split and toasted
- 12 oz. roasted chicken breast
- 8 slices lower-sodium, less-fat bacon, crisp cooked
- 4 slices fresh tomato
- 4 green leaf lettuce leaves

1. In a small bowl mash avocado with honey mustard until smooth. Spread cut sides of buns with avocado mixture. Fill buns with chicken, bacon, tomato, and lettuce.

Tip Cut two 8-oz. boneless, skinless chicken breast halves in half horizontally. Lightly coat a 10-inch skillet with nonstick cooking spray. Add chicken and cook over medium 8 to 10 minutes or until no longer pink (165°F), turning once.

To Tote Wrap sandwiches individually in plastic wrap. Place in insulated an lunch box. Add cooler pack or store lunch box in the refrigerator. Serve within 5 hours for best quality.

PER SERVING (1 sandwich each) **CAL** 387, **FAT** 12 g (4 g sat. fat), **CHOL** 104 mg, **SODIUM** 392 mg, **CARB** 29 g (2 g fiber, 11 g sugars), **PRO** 35 g

Chicken-Olive
Tabbouleh
Lettuce Wraps

Chicken-Olive Tabbouleh Lettuce Wraps

26 g
CARB

SERVES 2
HANDS ON 20 min.
TOTAL 6 hr. 35 min.

- ½ cup reduced-sodium chicken broth
- ¼ cup dry bulgur
- 2 Tbsp. purchased green olive tapenade
- 2 Tbsp. orange, tangerine, or mandarin orange juice
- 2 tsp. olive oil
- ½ cup orange, tangerine, or mandarin orange sections
- ¼ cup coarsely shredded carrot
- 2 green onions, thinly sliced
- 6 green or red leaf lettuce leaves
- 4 oz. cooked skinless, boneless chicken breast, shredded

1. In a small saucepan bring chicken broth to boiling. Place bulgur in a medium bowl. Pour broth over bulgur. Cover and let stand 15 minutes. If necessary, drain any excess broth.
2. Stir tapenade, orange juice, and oil into drained bulgur. Stir in orange sections, carrot, and green onion. Cover and chill 6 to 24 hours.
3. Spoon bulgur mixture onto lettuce leaves. Top with shredded chicken. Fold lettuce around filling to eat.

To Tote Place wraps in airtight containers and place containers upright in an insulated lunch box. Add cooler pack or store lunch box in the refrigerator. Serve within 5 hours for best quality.

PER SERVING (3 lettuce wraps each) **CAL** 263, **FAT** 8 g (1 g sat. fat), **CHOL** 48 mg, **SODIUM** 437 mg, **CARB** 26 g (5 g fiber, 8 g sugars), **PRO** 23 g

Chili-Cilantro Turkey Sandwiches

34 g
CARB

SERVES 4
TOTAL 25 min.

- 3 Tbsp. light mayonnaise
- 2 Tbsp. snipped fresh cilantro
- 1 tsp. hot or mild chili powder
- 8 slices very thinly sliced whole wheat bread or light whole wheat bread
- 4 oz. thinly sliced lower-sodium cooked turkey
- 4 slices reduced-fat cheddar cheese (3 oz. total)
- 1 medium fresh poblano pepper, stemmed, seeded, and thinly sliced crosswise (tip, p. 154)
- 1 medium fresh tomato, thinly sliced
- 4 cups mixed fresh berries

1. In a small bowl stir together mayonnaise, cilantro, and chili powder. Spread on bread slices.

2. Layer the next four ingredients (through tomato slices) on four of the bread slices; top with remaining bread slices. Serve sandwiches with berries.

To Tote Wrap tomato slices separately in plastic wrap. Wrap sandwich in plastic wrap or place in a sandwich container. Pack a sandwich, tomato slice, and berries in an insulated bag with ice packs. Place tomato slices on sandwiches just before eating.

PER SERVING *(1 sandwich each)* **CAL** 272, **FAT** 10 g (3 g sat. fat), **CHOL** 32 mg, **SODIUM** 612 mg, **CARB** 34 g (8 g fiber, 12 g sugars), **PRO** 16 g

Sloppy Turkey and Veggie Sandwiches

32 g
CARB

SERVES 6
TOTAL 25 min.

- 8 oz. uncooked ground turkey breast
- 2 cups chopped fresh cremini or button mushrooms
- ¾ cup chopped yellow or green sweet pepper
- ½ cup chopped onion
- 1 14.5-oz. can no-salt-added diced tomatoes with basil, garlic, and oregano, undrained
- 6 whole wheat hamburger buns, split and toasted
- 1 recipe Goat Cheese-Yogurt Sauce

1. In a 10-inch nonstick skillet cook turkey, mushrooms, sweet pepper, and onion over medium until turkey is browned and vegetables are tender. Stir in tomatoes. Cook over medium-low 5 minutes to blend flavors, stirring occasionally.

2. Fill buns with meat mixture. Spoon Goat Cheese-Yogurt Sauce over meat mixture.

Goat Cheese-Yogurt Sauce In a small microwave-safe bowl microwave **4 oz. soft goat cheese (chèvre)** about 10 seconds or until softened. Stir in **¼ cup snipped fresh chives; 1 clove garlic, minced; ⅛ tsp. salt;** and **⅛ tsp. black pepper.** Gradually stir in **one 6-oz. carton plain fat-free Greek yogurt** until smooth.

PER SERVING (1 sandwich each) **CAL** 263, **FAT** 5 g (3 g sat. fat), **CHOL** 27 mg, **SODIUM** 392 mg, **CARB** 32 g (7 g fiber, 11 g sugars), **PRO** 21 g

Sloppy Turkey and Veggie Sandwiches

Barbacoa Beef Tacos

34 g CARB

SERVES 8
HANDS ON 45 min.
TOTAL 3 hr.

- 1 cup reduced-sodium beef broth
- ½ of a 6-oz. can no-salt-added tomato paste
- ¼ cup cider vinegar
- 1 medium canned chipotle pepper in adobo sauce + 1 Tbsp. adobo sauce
- 4 cloves garlic, minced
- 2 tsp. ground cumin
- 1 tsp. dried oregano, crushed
- ¼ tsp. salt
- 1 2¼- to 2½-pound boneless beef chuck arm roast, trimmed and cut into 2-inch chunks
- 1 large onion, halved and thinly sliced
- 1 medium red sweet pepper, chopped
- 1 recipe Quick Pickled Onion
- 16 6-inch corn tortillas, warmed
- 4 cups shredded lettuce
- ½ cup light sour cream
- 1 cup fresh salsa
- ½ cup snipped fresh cilantro

Barbacoa Beef Tacos

1. Preheat oven to 325°F. For sauce, in a blender combine the first eight ingredients (through salt). Cover; blend until smooth.

2. Coat a 3½- to 4-qt. Dutch oven with *nonstick cooking spray;* heat over medium. Cook meat, half at a time, until browned, stirring occasionally. Return all beef to Dutch oven. Add onion and red pepper. Pour sauce over beef and vegetables. Bring to boiling; cover and place in oven. Bake about 2½ hours or until beef is very tender.

3. Remove meat from pot, reserving cooking liquid. Shred meat using two forks; discard fat. Skim fat from cooking liquid. Bring cooking liquid to simmering over medium. Simmer about 5 minutes or until liquid is reduced by half. Return meat to Dutch oven; toss to coat.

4. While beef is baking, prepare Quick Pickled Onion. Drain onion before serving. To serve, top tortillas with beef, onion, and the remaining ingredients.

Quick Pickled Onion Place **1½ cups slivered red onion** in a bowl. Add **½ cup lime juice** and sprinkle with **¼ tsp. salt**; toss. Press onion with the back of a fork to submerge. Cover and chill at least 2 hours or up to 3 days. Drain before serving.

PER SERVING *(2 tacos each)* **CAL** 347, **FAT** 9 g (3 g sat. fat), **CHOL** 87 mg, **SODIUM** 432 mg, **CARB** 34 g (6 g fiber, 8 g sugars), **PRO** 33 g

Open-Face Meatball Subs with Caramelized Onions

29 g
CARB

SERVES 4
HANDS ON 40 min.
TOTAL 1 hr.

Nonstick cooking spray
1 large sweet onion, cut into thin wedges (about 1½ cups)
1 12-oz. jar roasted red sweet peppers, drained
2 tsp. balsamic vinegar
2 crusty kaiser, french, or hoagie rolls

1 recipe Sandwich Meatballs
½ cup shredded part-skim mozzarella cheese (2 oz.)

1. Coat a 10-inch nonstick skillet with cooking spray; heat skillet over medium-low. Add onion wedges. Cook, covered, 15 minutes, stirring occasionally. Uncover; increase heat to medium-high. Cook 5 to 10 minutes more or until onions are golden brown, stirring occasionally.

2. Transfer half of the onions to a blender. Add roasted peppers and vinegar. Cover; blend until smooth, scraping sides of blender as needed.

3. Preheat oven to 425°F. Line a baking sheet with foil; coat foil with cooking spray. Split rolls horizontally. Hollow out centers. Place roll halves on the prepared baking sheet. Bake about 6 minutes or until lightly toasted.

4. Spoon Sandwich Meatballs into roll halves. Top meatballs with blended sauce, the remaining caramelized onions, and the cheese. Bake 5 to 8 minutes or until heated and cheese is melted.

Sandwich Meatballs Preheat oven to 350°F. Line a baking pan with foil. In a bowl combine **1 egg, lightly beaten; ¼ cup whole wheat panko bread crumbs; 1 tsp. dried Italian seasoning; 2 cloves garlic, minced;** and **¼ tsp. black pepper.** Add **12 oz. lean ground beef (90% lean);** mix well. Shape mixture into 16 meatballs. Arrange meatballs in the prepared pan. Bake 20 to 25 minutes or until done (160°F). Drain meatballs on paper towels.

PER SERVING *(1 sandwich each)* **CAL** 346, **FAT** 13 g (5 g sat. fat), **CHOL** 109 mg, **SODIUM** 466 mg, **CARB** 29 g (3 g fiber, 6 g sugars), **PRO** 26 g

Beef Gyros

19 g CARB

SERVES 8
HANDS ON 30 min.
TOTAL 1 hr. 15 min.

Nonstick cooking spray
1 cup chopped onion
2 tablespoons water
1 pound lean ground beef (95% lean)
1 egg
¼ cup dry whole wheat bread crumbs
4 tsp. dried oregano, crushed
2 tsp. dried marjoram, crushed
3 cloves garlic, minced
½ tsp. kosher salt
½ tsp. black pepper

8 low-carb pita bread rounds
3 medium roma tomatoes, sliced
½ cup thinly sliced cucumber
¼ cup thinly sliced red onion
½ cup crumbled reduced-fat feta cheese (2 oz.)
1 recipe Tzatziki Sauce

1. Preheat oven to 325°F. Line a 9×5-inch loaf pan with parchment paper; coat paper with cooking spray.
2. In a food processor combine the 1 cup onion and the water; cover and process until smooth. Press pureed onion through a fine-mesh sieve to remove excess liquid; discard liquid. Return onion to food processor. Add the next eight ingredients (through pepper). Cover and process until mixture forms a paste.
3. Lightly press meat mixture into prepared loaf pan. Place loaf pan in a 13×9-inch baking pan. Add boiling water to baking pan to reach halfway up sides of loaf pan. Bake 35 to 40 minutes or until done (160°F). Drain fat. Cool 10 minutes. Remove loaf from pan; cut into slices about ¼ inch thick.
4. Fill pita bread with meat, tomato, cucumber, and red onion slices; top with feta. Serve with Tzatziki Sauce.

Tzatziki Sauce In a small bowl stir together **half of a 6-oz. carton plain fat-free Greek yogurt; ½ cup shredded, seeded cucumber; 1½ tsp. each snipped fresh dill and red wine vinegar; 1 clove garlic, minced; and ¼ tsp. kosher salt.** If desired, cover and chill up to 4 hours before serving. Makes about ¾ cup.

Tip The meat may appear a bit pink after baking, so be sure to use an instant-read thermometer to check doneness.

PER SERVING (1 sandwich each) **CAL** 206, **FAT** 7 g (2 g sat. fat), **CHOL** 64 mg, **SODIUM** 610 mg, **CARB** 19 g (7 g fiber, 4 g sugars), **PRO** 24 g

Beef Gyros

Roast Beef, Arugula, and Pickled Onion Wrap

32 g CARB

SERVES 1
HANDS ON 15 min.
TOTAL 8 hr. 15 min.

2 Tbsp. cider vinegar
1 tsp. honey
Dash salt
¼ cup very thinly sliced red onion
1 8-inch low-carb whole wheat flour tortilla
1 Tbsp. mango chutney
2 oz. thinly sliced reduced-sodium cooked roast beef
1 cup arugula

1. In a bowl combine vinegar, honey, and salt. Stir in onion. Cover and chill overnight.

**Roast Beef, Arugula,
and Pickled Onion Wrap**

2. Spread tortilla with chutney and top with meat and arugula. Drain onion, discarding liquid. Spoon onion over arugula. Roll up tortilla around filling.

For 4 To serve four, use ½ cup cider vinegar, 1 Tbsp. honey, ⅛ tsp. salt,

1 cup onion, 4 tortillas, ¼ cup chutney, 8 oz. roast beef, and 4 cups arugula.

To Tote Wrap sandwich in plastic wrap. Place in an insulated lunch box. Add cooler pack or store lunch box in the refrigerator.

PER SERVING (*1 sandwich*) **CAL** 239, **FAT** 5 g (2 g sat. fat), **CHOL** 40 mg, **SODIUM** 572 mg, **CARB** 32 g (8 g fiber, 17 g sugars), **PRO** 21 g

BLTs with Creamy
Tomato-Avocado
Spread

BLTs with Creamy Tomato-Avocado Spread

20 g
CARB

SERVES 4
TOTAL 30 min.

- 6 dried tomatoes (not oil-packed)
  Boiling water
- 12 slices lower-sodium, less-fat bacon, halved crosswise
- 1 small avocado, halved, seeded, and peeled
- ¼ cup reduced-fat semisoft cheese with garlic and fines herbes, such as Alouette brand
- 8 very thin slices whole wheat bread, toasted
- 2 medium orange, red, and/or yellow tomatoes, thickly sliced
- 1 cup watercress or fresh spinach leaves

1. In a bowl combine dried tomatoes and enough boiling water to cover. Let stand, covered, 5 minutes. Drain and chop tomatoes. Meanwhile, in a 10-inch skillet cook bacon over medium until browned. Drain on paper towels.

2. In a medium bowl mash avocado. Stir in chopped tomatoes and cheese.
3. To assemble, spread half of the bread slices with avocado mixture. Layer with bacon, sliced tomatoes, and watercress. Add remaining bread slices.

PER SERVING (1 sandwich each) **CAL** 230, **FAT** 11 g (4 g sat. fat), **CHOL** 18 mg, **SODIUM** 454 mg, **CARB** 20 g (5 g fiber, 5 g sugars), **PRO** 11 g

Ginger-Plum Pulled Pork Sandwiches with Sesame Slaw

28 g
CARB

SERVES 8
HANDS ON 30 min.
SLOW COOK 9 hr.

- 1 2½- to 3-lb. boneless pork shoulder
- 2 tsp. ground coriander
- 1 tsp. ground ginger
- ½ tsp. salt
- ½ tsp. ground allspice
- ¼ tsp. black pepper
- 1 Tbsp. canola oil
- 1 medium onion, cut into thin wedges
- 8 dried pitted plums (prunes)
- ½ cup reduced-sodium chicken broth
- 8 whole wheat reduced-calorie hamburger buns, split and toasted
- 1 recipe Sesame Slaw

1. Cut roast into three equal portions. Trim all visible fat from meat. In a bowl combine the next five ingredients (through pepper). Sprinkle over all roast portions, rubbing in with your fingers. In a 12-inch skillet heat oil over medium. Add roast portions and cook 8 to 10 minutes or until meat is browned, turning to evenly brown all sides.
2. Place onion wedges, prunes, and broth in a 3½- or 4-qt. slow cooker. Top with browned roast portions. Cover and cook on low 9 to 10 hours or on high 4½ to 5 hours.
3. Transfer meat to a cutting board. Shred meat using two forks; discard any fat. Skim fat from cooking liquid. Measure 1 cup of the cooking liquid; discard any remaining cooking liquid. Transfer the 1 cup cooking liquid, the onion, and prunes to a blender. Cover; blend until smooth. Return to cooker with shredded pork; toss with tongs to combine.
4. Serve meat in buns with some of the Sesame Slaw. Pass any remaining slaw to serve on the side.

Sesame Slaw In a medium bowl toss together **4 cups shredded cabbage with carrot (coleslaw mix)** and **½ cup thinly sliced green onions.** In a screw-top jar combine **2 Tbsp. each vinegar and honey, 1 Tbsp. each sesame seeds and canola oil,** and **2 tsp. sesame oil.** Cover; shake well. Drizzle over cabbage mixture; toss to coat. Serve immediately or cover and chill up to 4 hours.

PER SERVING (1 sandwich each) **CAL** 367, **FAT** 14 g (3 g sat. fat), **CHOL** 85 mg, **SODIUM** 443 mg, **CARB** 28 g (8 g fiber, 12 g sugars), **PRO** 32 g

QUICK TIP For 4, freeze half of the pork in an airtight container up to 3 months and make half as much slaw.

Ginger-Plum Pulled Pork Sandwiches with Sesame Slaw

Shrimp Lettuce Rolls

½ cup of the celery, ¼ cup of the fennel, the wine, bay leaf, and garlic. Bring to boiling. Stir in shrimp; reduce heat. Simmer, covered, 3 to 4 minutes or until shrimp are opaque. Remove shrimp; cool. Coarsely chop shrimp.

3. In a blender or food processor combine the next six ingredients (through mustard). Cover and blend or process until smooth. In a medium bowl combine chopped shrimp, the remaining ½ cup celery and ¼ cup fennel, and the carrot. Stir in tofu mixture. Spoon onto lettuce leaves and top with croutons and fennel fronds.

PER SERVING *(2 lettuce rolls each)* **CAL** 197, **FAT** 7 g (2 g sat. fat), **CHOL** 169 mg, **SODIUM** 359 mg, **CARB** 9 g (1 g fiber, 3 g sugars), **PRO** 23 g

Shrimp Lettuce Rolls

9g
CARB

SERVES 4
TOTAL 45 min.

- 1 lb. fresh or frozen medium shrimp in shells
- 1 cup ¼- to ½-inch cubes Italian bread (1 oz.)
- 1 Tbsp. butter, melted
  Black pepper
- 1 cup water
- 1 cup finely chopped celery
- ½ cup finely chopped fennel bulb
- ½ cup dry white wine or 2 Tbsp. lemon juice
- 1 bay leaf
- 1 clove garlic, sliced
- ½ of a 12-oz. pkg. soft, silken-style tofu
- 2 Tbsp. light mayonnaise
- 1 Tbsp. cider vinegar
- 1 tsp. reduced-sodium seafood seasoning
- 1 tsp. honey
- ½ tsp. Dijon-style mustard
- ¼ cup shredded carrot
- 8 small butterhead lettuce leaves
- 2 Tbsp. coarsely snipped fennel fronds

1. Preheat oven to 300°F. Thaw shrimp, if frozen. For croutons, in a bowl drizzle bread with melted butter and sprinkle with pepper; toss to coat. Spread in a 15×10-inch baking pan. Bake about 30 minutes or until bread is golden and crisp, stirring once. Cool in pan on a wire rack.

2. Meanwhile, peel and devein shrimp. Rinse shrimp; pat dry. In a large saucepan combine the water,

Asparagus-Egg Sandwiches

34g
CARB

SERVES 2
TOTAL 10 min.

- 4 slices whole wheat bread, toasted
- 1 tsp. Dijon-style mustard
- 1 avocado, seeded, peeled, and mashed
- 8 to 12 asparagus spears, steamed
- 1 hard-cooked egg, sliced
- ⅛ tsp. coarse sea salt
- ⅛ tsp. cracked black pepper

1. Spread two toast slices with mustard. Spread remaining two toast slices with mashed avocado. Top with asparagus spears and egg slices. Sprinkle with salt and black pepper. Top with mustard-coated toast slices.

To Make Ahead Hard-cook the eggs and steam the asparagus ahead of time. Cover and refrigerate asparagus up to 5 days and eggs up to 7 days.

PER SERVING *(1 sandwich each)* **CAL** 317, **FAT** 15 g (3 g sat. fat), **CHOL** 93 mg, **SODIUM** 518 mg, **CARB** 34 g (10 g fiber, 5 g sugars), **PRO** 14 g

**Asparagus-Egg
Sandwiches**

Grilled Vegetable
Quesadillas

Mediterranean Sandwich

38 g
CARB

SERVES 1

TOTAL 15 min.

½ cup canned no-salt-added
garbanzo beans (chickpeas),
rinsed and drained
1 Tbsp. lemon juice
¼ tsp. ground cumin
⅛ tsp. black pepper
Dash salt
½ whole wheat pita bread round
1 Tbsp. finely chopped red onion
2 Tbsp. chopped cucumber
1 Tbsp. crumbled reduced-fat
feta cheese
2 slices roma tomato

1. In a bowl coarsely mash the first
five ingredients (through salt). Gently
open pita bread to make pocket. Stuff
with bean mixture and the remaining
ingredients.

To Tote Prepare as directed, except
do not add tomato. Wrap sandwich in
plastic wrap or place in a covered
container. Place tomato in a separate
container. Pack containers in an
insulated bag with ice packs. Before
eating, place tomato on sandwich.

PER SERVING (1 sandwich) **CAL** 206,
FAT 3 g (1 g sat. fat), **CHOL** 3 mg,
SODIUM 461 mg, **CARB** 38 g (7 g fiber,
4 g sugars), **PRO** 10 g

Grilled Vegetable Quesadillas

36 g
CARB

SERVES 2

TOTAL 30 min.

1 ear of corn, husked
¼ of a fresh poblano chile pepper
(tip, p. 154) or green sweet
pepper
¼ of a yellow summer squash, cut
lengthwise into ¼-inch slices
1 ¼-inch slice red onion
Nonstick cooking spray
¼ tsp. black pepper
2 7-inch low-carb flour tortillas
½ cup shredded reduced-fat
Mexican cheese blend (2 oz.)
½ cup pico de gallo
¼ cup plain fat-free Greek yogurt
Fresh cilantro leaves (optional)

1. Lightly coat the first four
ingredients (through onion) with
cooking spray. Grill corn and poblano

pepper, covered, over medium
4 minutes. Add onion; grill, covered,
5 minutes. Add squash; grill, covered,
about 3 minutes more or until
vegetables are tender and lightly
charred, turning corn frequently and
pepper, onion, and squash once.
2. Cut corn kernels off cob. Coarsely
chop poblano pepper, onion, and
squash. Sprinkle vegetables with
black pepper. Spoon vegetables
onto tortillas just below centers;
sprinkle with cheese. Fold tortillas
in half over filling. Coat with cooking
spray; press lightly.
3. Grill quesadillas, covered, over
medium 3 to 4 minutes or until golden
and crisp, carefully turning once. Cut
into quarters. Serve with the remaining
ingredients.

PER SERVING (1 quesadilla each) **CAL** 277,
FAT 9 g (5 g sat. fat), **CHOL** 18 mg,
SODIUM 538 mg, **CARB** 36 g (15 g fiber,
7 g sugars), **PRO** 17 g

Mediterranean
Sandwich

Tofu and Pickled Vegetable Sandwiches

47 g
CARB

SERVES 4
TOTAL 45 min.

3 cups thinly sliced cucumbers, radishes, and carrots
1 shallot, very thinly sliced
1 Tbsp. rice vinegar or cider vinegar
⅛ tsp. sugar
Dash salt
16 oz. firm tofu, drained and cut crosswise into 8 slices

¼ cup light mayonnaise
2 tsp. sriracha sauce
1 Tbsp. lime juice
4 hoagie rolls, split and toasted
½ cup fresh cilantro leaves

1. For pickled vegetables, in a medium bowl combine the first five ingredients (through salt); let stand at least 15 minutes, stirring occasionally.
2. Wrap tofu with paper towels; press firmly to squeeze out excess moisture. In a bowl stir together mayonnaise and sriracha. Spread half the mixture in a thin layer on one side of tofu slices.

3. Heat a 12-inch nonstick skillet over medium-high. Add tofu slices, mayonnaise-mixture side down; cook 4 to 6 minutes or until golden brown, turning once. Remove pan from heat. Drizzle tofu with lime juice.
4. Spread rolls with remaining mayonnaise mixture. Top with tofu, drained pickled vegetables, and cilantro.

PER SERVING (1 sandwich each) **CAL** 345, **FAT** 10 g (1 g sat. fat), **CHOL** 2 mg, **SODIUM** 658 mg, **CARB** 47 g (5 g fiber, 7 g sugars), **PRO** 19 g

TASTY TOAST TOPPERS

Toast toppers are all the rage, and for good reason: They're a tasty option for using up leftovers. Chow down on these healthful slices with a side of your choice for a full meal or enjoy as a light breakfast.

SHOP SMART. Look for bread brands with fewer than 19 grams of carbohydrate and under 100 calories per slice. Always pick whole grain breads to ensure you're getting at least 3 grams of good-for-you fiber.

Caprese Toast

Top **1 slice toast** with **1½ oz. fresh mozzarella, thinly sliced**; **3 thin slices tomato**; **1 Tbsp. thinly sliced fresh basil**; and **1 tsp. bottled light balsamic vinaigrette salad dressing**. Sprinkle with **cracked black pepper**.

SERVES 1. CAL 243, CARB 25 g (3 g fiber, 3 g sugars)

Goat Cheese, Blackberry, and Almond Toast

Spread **½ oz. goat cheese (chèvre)** onto **1 slice toast**. Top with **2 Tbsp. blackberries**, **1 Tbsp. sliced almonds**, and **1 tsp. honey**.

SERVES 1. CAL 242, CARB 32 g (5 g fiber, 9 g sugars)

Greek Salmon Toast

Spread **1 Tbsp. reduced-fat cream cheese (neufchatel)**, softened, onto **1 slice toast**. Top with **4 thin slices cucumber**; **½ of a 2.5-oz. pouch skinless, boneless pink salmon, coarsely flaked**; **1 Tbsp. finely chopped red onion**; and **½ tsp. snipped fresh dill weed**.

SERVES 1. CAL 207, CARB 26 g (3 g fiber, 3 g sugars)

Cheddar and Roasted Corn Toast

Top **1 slice toast** with **1 Tbsp. canned fire-roasted corn**, **1 Tbsp. reduced-sodium black beans**, and **1 thin slice sharp cheddar cheese.** Broil until cheese is melted. Top with **1 Tbsp. low-sodium salsa,** such as Newman's Own.

SERVES 1. **CAL** 201, **CARB** 30 g (4 g fiber, 3 g sugars)

Hummus, Red Pepper, and Feta Toast

Spread **3 Tbsp. hummus** onto **1 slice toast.** Top with **2 Tbsp. sliced fire-roasted red sweet peppers, 1 Tbsp. crumbled reduced-fat feta cheese,** and **1 Tbsp. snipped fresh basil.**

SERVES 1. **CAL** 235, **CARB** 35 g (5 g fiber, 3 g sugars)

Peanut Butter and Apple-Cinnamon Toast

Spread **4 tsp. creamy peanut butter** onto **1 slice toast.** Top with **¼ of an apple, cored and sliced,** and **a pinch ground cinnamon.**

SERVES 1. **CAL** 252, **CARB** 33 g (5 g fiber, 8 g sugars)

White Bean Toast

Top **1 slice toast** with **⅓ cup canned no-salt-added cannellini (white kidney) beans, rinsed and drained; ½ tsp. basil pesto; a pinch garlic powder;** and **2 Tbsp. chopped tomato.**

SERVES 1. **CAL** 212, **CARB** 36 g (7 g fiber, 3 g sugars)

SIMPLE
SIDES & SALADS

5

Complement your main dish with tasty and nutritious side dishes and side salads that won't break your daily carb budget. Pair Sautéed Cabbage and Bacon with roasted pork loin, Grilled Polenta and Greens with grilled chicken breast, and Basil and Olive Potatoes with broiled Italian-herbed beef steak.

QUICK TIP ⌄

Save a little time by substituting packaged shredded cabbage with carrot (coleslaw mix) for the sliced green cabbage.

Sautéed Cabbage with Bacon

Sautéed Cabbage with Bacon

10 g CARB

SERVES 4
TOTAL 20 min.

- 2 slices lower-sodium, less-fat bacon, chopped
- 4 cups thinly sliced green cabbage
- 1 medium red sweet pepper, cut into bite-size strips
- 1 onion, halved and thinly sliced
- 2 Tbsp. water
- 2 Tbsp. light mayonnaise
- 1 Tbsp. coarse-ground mustard
- 1 Tbsp. cider vinegar
- ¼ tsp. caraway seeds, crushed
- ⅛ tsp. celery seeds

1. In a 10-inch nonstick skillet cook bacon over medium about 5 minutes or until cooked through, stirring occasionally. Remove bacon from skillet. Add cabbage, sweet pepper, onion, and the water to skillet. Cover and cook over medium about 5 minutes or until vegetables are just tender, stirring occasionally.
2. In a small bowl combine the next five ingredients (through celery seeds). Add to cabbage mixture in skillet. Toss until well coated. Sprinkle with cooked bacon. Serve warm.

PER SERVING (¾ cup each) **CAL** 74, **FAT** 3 g (1 g sat. fat), **CHOL** 3 mg, **SODIUM** 162 mg, **CARB** 10 g (3 g fiber, 5 g sugars), **PRO** 3 g

Baked Root Vegetable Chips

Baked Root Vegetable Chips

13 g CARB

SERVES 4
HANDS ON 15 min.
TOTAL 40 min.

- Nonstick cooking spray
- 2 sweet potatoes, purple beets, and/or golden beets, peeled
- ¼ tsp. salt
- ¼ tsp. black pepper

1. Preheat oven to 375°F. Lightly coat two large baking sheets with cooking spray.
2. Use a mandoline to slice vegetables as thin as possible. (If using beets, sandwich slices between layers of paper towels and press firmly to remove excess liquid.) Arrange vegetable slices in a single layer on the prepared baking sheets. Coat tops of vegetable slices with cooking spray; sprinkle with salt and pepper.

3. Bake 10 minutes. Remove baking sheets from oven and let stand 5 minutes. Return baking sheets to oven. Bake 4 to 8 minutes more, removing baking sheets to check for doneness every minute after 4 minutes. Chips are done when centers of chips no longer look wet. Transfer chips to paper towels. Let cool 5 minutes to crisp the chips.

Tip To avoid burning chips, check the doneness frequently and remove each type of chip when done.

To Store Place cooled chips in an airtight container and store up to 24 hours. If necessary, recrisp the chips by baking them in a 325°F oven 3 to 4 minutes.

PER SERVING (¼ of the chips each) **CAL** 56, **FAT** 0 g, **CHOL** 0 mg, **SODIUM** 181 mg, **CARB** 13 g (2 g fiber, 3 g sugars), **PRO** 1 g

Orzo with Mint, Peas, and Parmesan

Farro-Chard Stuffed Portobellos

22 g
CARB

SERVES	6
HANDS ON	30 min.
TOTAL	1 hr. 20 min.

- 1½ cups water
- ½ cup farro
- 6 4-inch-diameter portobello mushrooms, stems removed Olive oil nonstick cooking spray
- ¼ tsp. freshly cracked black pepper
- 2 tsp. olive oil
- ⅔ cup thinly sliced leeks
- ⅓ cup chopped dried tomatoes
- 3 Tbsp. snipped fresh basil
- 6 cloves garlic, minced
- 2 tsp. snipped fresh thyme leaves
- 8 ounces Swiss chard, stemmed and coarsely chopped (3 cups)
- 6 ounces fresh mozzarella pearls
- 1 Tbsp. balsamic vinegar

1. Preheat oven to 400°F. In a large saucepan bring water to boiling. Stir in farro; reduce heat. Simmer, covered, about 25 minutes or until tender. Drain.
2. Meanwhile, line a large baking sheet with parchment paper or foil. Coat both sides of mushroom caps lightly with cooking spray. Sprinkle stem sides of mushrooms with pepper. Arrange mushrooms, stem sides up, on the prepared baking sheet. Bake about 15 minutes or until mushrooms are just tender.
3. In a 10-inch nonstick skillet heat oil over medium. Add the next five ingredients (through thyme). Cook and stir 4 to 5 minutes or until leeks are tender. Gradually stir in chard. Cook and stir 2 to 3 minutes or until chard wilts. Remove from heat. Stir in mozzarella, farro, and vinegar.
4. Fill mushroom caps with chard mixture. Bake about 10 minutes or until heated through.

PER SERVING *(1 stuffed mushroom each)* **CAL** 196, **FAT** 7 g (3 g sat. fat), **CHOL** 20 mg, **SODIUM** 198 mg, **CARB** 22 g (4 g fiber, 5 g sugars), **PRO** 11 g

Orzo with Mint, Peas, and Parmesan

24 g
CARB

SERVES	6
TOTAL	25 min.

- 1 cup dried orzo pasta (6 oz.)
- 1½ cups fresh sugar snap pea pods, sliced diagonally
- 1 lemon
- ⅓ cup freshly shredded Parmesan cheese
- ¼ cup snipped fresh mint
- 2 Tbsp. pine nuts, toasted
- 1 Tbsp. olive oil
- 1 tsp. white wine vinegar
- ¼ tsp. salt

1. Cook orzo according to package directions, adding snap peas the last 1 minute; drain. Rinse with cold water; drain again.
2. Meanwhile, remove 1 tsp. zest and squeeze 2 Tbsp. juice from lemon. In a medium bowl combine lemon zest and juice and the remaining ingredients. Add orzo mixture, stirring to coat. If desired, cover and chill up to 4 hours before serving.

Tip Chill up to 24 hours, but leave out the mint until ready to serve.

PER SERVING *(½ cup each)* **CAL** 173, **FAT** 6 g (1 g sat. fat), **CHOL** 3 mg, **SODIUM** 176 mg, **CARB** 24 g (2 g fiber, 2 g sugars), **PRO** 6 g

Farro-Chard
Stuffed Portobellos

Grilled Polenta and Greens

Grilled Polenta and Greens

17 g CARB

SERVES	10
HANDS ON	40 min.
TOTAL	2 hr. 10 min.

2½ cups water
1 cup yellow cornmeal
¾ cup cold water
1 tsp. kosher salt
1 tsp. ground cumin
¼ cup bulgur
¼ cup finely chopped green onions
4 Tbsp. olive oil
3 Tbsp. lemon juice
1 cup arugula
1 cup fresh raspberries
½ of a medium cucumber, chopped
½ cup chopped fresh Italian parsley
½ cup chopped fresh mint
¼ cup crumbled feta cheese

1. Line a 9-inch round cake pan with plastic wrap. In a medium saucepan bring 2½ cups water to boiling. Meanwhile, in a bowl stir together the cornmeal, ¾ cup cold water, salt, and cumin. Slowly add cornmeal mixture to boiling water, stirring constantly. Reduce heat to medium-low. Cook and stir about 15 minutes or until very thick. Remove from heat and stir in bulgur and green onions. Spread in prepared cake pan. Let stand, uncovered, 30 minutes. Cover and chill at least 1 hour or until firm.
2. Remove polenta from pan; remove plastic wrap. Pat dry with paper towels. Brush both sides with 1 Tbsp. of the olive oil. Grill polenta, covered, over medium about 15 minutes or until charred and heated, turning once using a flat baking sheet.
3. In a large bowl whisk together remaining 3 Tbsp. oil and the lemon juice. Add the next five ingredients (through mint). Place polenta on a platter. Top with salad and sprinkle with feta.

PER SERVING (1 wedge polenta + ½ cup salad each) **CAL** 136, **FAT** 7 g (1 g sat. fat), **CHOL** 3 mg, **SODIUM** 155 mg, **CARB** 17 g (2 g fiber, 1 g sugars), **PRO** 3 g

Sheet-Pan Succotash

Sheet-Pan Succotash

12 g CARB

SERVES	8
TOTAL	30 min.

12 oz. okra, halved lengthwise
2 chopped orange, yellow, and/or red sweet peppers
1 10- to 12-oz. pkg. frozen shelled edamame
¼ cup olive oil
1 tsp. salt
16 oz. cherry tomatoes, halved
¼ cup chopped fresh dill weed
2 Tbsp. apple cider vinegar

1. Preheat oven to 450°F. Heat a 15×10-inch pan in hot oven 10 minutes. Meanwhile, in a large bowl combine the first five ingredients (through salt). Transfer to the heated pan.
2. Roast 20 to 25 minutes or until just tender, adding cherry tomatoes the last 5 minutes. Remove from oven. Stir in dill weed and apple cider vinegar.

PER SERVING (1 cup each) **CAL** 140, **FAT** 9 g (1 g sat. fat), **CHOL** 0 mg, **SODIUM** 300 mg, **CARB** 12 g (4 g fiber, 4 g sugars), **PRO** 6 g

Basil and Olive Potatoes

18 g CARB

SERVES 10
TOTAL 40 min.

- 2 lb. small new potatoes, quartered
- ¼ cup canola oil
- 1½ cups fresh basil leaves
- 3 cloves garlic, minced
- ⅓ cup white wine vinegar
- 2 Tbsp. lemon juice
- 2 Tbsp. light mayonnaise
- ¼ tsp. salt
- ½ tsp. black pepper
- 2 large yellow sweet peppers
- ½ cup green Castelvetrano olives or other green olives, pitted

1. In a large pot combine potatoes and enough cold water to cover. Bring to boiling; reduce heat. Cover and cook about 10 minutes or until just tender.
2. Meanwhile, in a small saucepan combine oil, ½ cup of the basil, and the garlic. Heat over medium-low. Drain potatoes. Remove oil from heat and remove basil. In a blender combine the oil and the next five ingredients (through black pepper). Cover and blend until smooth. Transfer potatoes to serving bowl. Pour dressing over potatoes and gently toss to coat; cover and set aside.
3. Grill sweet peppers, covered, over medium 7 to 10 minutes or until charred, turning occasionally. Remove and cool slightly. Halve peppers, removing stems and seeds. Cut into large pieces. Add to potato mixture along with olives. Toss in remaining 1 cup basil. Serve warm or at room temperature.

PER SERVING (¾ cup each) **CAL** 145, **FAT** 7 g (1 g sat. fat), **CHOL** 0 mg, **SODIUM** 214 mg, **CARB** 18 g (3 g fiber, 3 g sugars), **PRO** 2 g

Basil and Olive Potatoes

Simply Scalloped Potatoes

24 g **SERVES** 8
CARB **HANDS ON** 25 min.
TOTAL 1 hr. 25 min.

Nonstick cooking spray
3 cups thinly sliced, peeled red potatoes
2 cups thinly sliced, peeled sweet potatoes
1 shallot, thinly sliced
2 Tbsp. butter
1 Tbsp. all-purpose flour
1 12-oz. can evaporated fat-free milk
1 tsp. snipped fresh thyme leaves
2 cloves garlic, minced
¼ tsp. black pepper
½ cup finely shredded Parmesan cheese (2 oz.)

1. Preheat oven to 375°F. Coat a 1½-qt. oval baking dish or casserole with cooking spray. Arrange potato slices and shallot slices in the prepared baking dish.
2. In a small saucepan melt butter over medium. Stir in flour. Cook and stir 30 seconds. Whisk in the next four ingredients (through pepper). Heat and stir until thickened and bubbly. Stir in half of the cheese. Pour over potatoes in baking dish.
3. Bake, covered, 35 minutes. Sprinkle with the remaining cheese. Bake, uncovered, about 15 minutes more or until potatoes are tender and top is lightly browned. Let stand 10 minutes before serving. If desired, top with additional snipped fresh thyme.

PER SERVING (about ¾ cup each) **CAL** 162, **FAT** 4 g (3 g sat. fat), **CHOL** 11 mg, **SODIUM** 197 mg, **CARB** 24 g (2 g fiber, 8 g sugars), **PRO** 7 g

Strawberry, Avocado,
and Arugula Salad

Strawberry, Avocado, and Arugula Salad

15 g
CARB

SERVES 6
TOTAL 20 min.

- 2 cups quartered fresh strawberries
- 2 Tbsp. olive oil
- 2 Tbsp. honey
- 1½ Tbsp. white wine vinegar
- ¼ tsp. salt
- 1 5-oz. pkg. fresh baby arugula
- 1 avocado, halved, seeded, peeled, and chopped
- ½ cup thinly sliced red onion
- ¼ cup crumbled reduced-fat feta cheese (1 oz.)

1. For dressing, in a blender combine 1 cup of the strawberries, the oil, honey, vinegar, and salt. Cover and blend until smooth. If desired, cover and chill up to 48 hours.
2. Arrange arugula on a large platter. Top with the remaining 1 cup strawberries, the avocado, and onion. Drizzle with dressing and sprinkle with cheese.

PER SERVING (1 cup each) **CAL** 141, **FAT** 9 g (1 g sat. fat), **CHOL** 2 mg, **SODIUM** 164 mg, **CARB** 15 g (3 g fiber, 11 g sugars), **PRO** 2 g

Two-Tone Bean Salad with Hazelnuts and Parmesan

Two-Tone Bean Salad with Hazelnuts and Parmesan

7 g
CARB

SERVES 12
TOTAL 30 min.

- ¼ cup olive oil
- 3 Tbsp. lemon juice
- 4 cloves garlic, minced
- 1 tsp. Dijon-style mustard
- ¼ tsp. salt
- ⅛ tsp. black pepper
- 2 lb. fresh green and wax beans, trimmed and cut diagonally into ½-inch pieces
- ½ cup hazelnuts (filberts), toasted and chopped
  Shaved Parmesan cheese

1. For dressing, in a small bowl whisk together the first six ingredients (through pepper).
2. In a large saucepan cook beans, covered, in a small amount of boiling salted water 8 to 10 minutes or until crisp-tender; drain. Immediately plunge beans into ice water; let stand 3 minutes. Drain well.
3. Transfer beans to a serving bowl. Whisk dressing again; pour over beans. Toss gently to coat. Top with hazelnuts and cheese.

Tip No yellow beans? Use all green. Out of hazelnuts? Use toasted walnuts instead. Prefer another vegetable? Tear the leaves from two large bunches of kale in place of the beans and skip Step 2 to make a raw kale salad.

PER SERVING (about ⅔ cup each) **CAL** 105, **FAT** 8 g (1 g sat. fat), **CHOL** 2 mg, **SODIUM** 101 mg, **CARB** 7 g (3 g fiber, 3 g sugars), **PRO** 3 g

Avocado and Caramelized Pineapple Salad

15 g CARB

SERVES 12
TOTAL 40 min.

- 2 Tbsp. sugar
- ½ tsp. hot chili powder
- 1 fresh pineapple, peeled, cored, and cut into 1-inch-thick slices
- ⅓ cup olive oil
- ⅓ cup white wine vinegar
- ⅓ cup orange juice
- ¼ cup snipped fresh cilantro leaves
- 2 cloves garlic, minced
- 1 tsp. kosher salt
- ¼ tsp. black pepper
- 1 medium red onion, coarsely chopped
- 1 large yellow or red sweet pepper, cut into 1-inch pieces
- 3 firm, ripe avocados, halved, seeded, peeled, and cut into 1-inch pieces
- 1 cup blackberries, rinsed and drained
- 2 cups chopped romaine lettuce

1. In a small bowl combine sugar and chili powder. Sprinkle evenly over pineapple slices. In a 12-inch nonstick skillet cook pineapple slices over medium-high 8 to 10 minutes or until golden brown, turning once. Remove from heat. Cool 10 minutes. Cut pineapple slices into 1-inch pieces.

2. In a large bowl whisk together the next seven ingredients (through black pepper). Add pineapple and the next four ingredients (through blackberries). Toss gently to combine. Add lettuce. Toss gently until mixture is just coated.

PER SERVING *(1¼ cups each)* **CAL** 162, **FAT** 11 g (2 g sat. fat), **CHOL** 0 mg, **SODIUM** 194 mg, **CARB** 15 g (4 g fiber, 8 g sugars), **PRO** 2 g

Confetti Corn Salad

17 g CARB

SERVES 10
TOTAL 30 min.

- 6 ears fresh corn, husked
- 1 cup canned unsweetened light coconut milk
- 1 green onion, thinly sliced
- ¼ cup lime juice
- 1 tsp. ground turmeric
- ½ tsp. kosher salt
- 2 cups chopped red sweet peppers
- 1 cup chopped cantaloupe
- ¾ cup roasted, salted cashews
- ¼ cup unsweetened coconut flakes, toasted
- ½ cup corn nuts (optional)

1. Cut kernels from corn cobs. You should have about 3 cups.

2. In a large bowl, whisk together the next five ingredients (through salt). Add corn, sweet peppers, cantaloupe, and cashews. Toss to coat. Sprinkle with toasted coconut and, if desired, corn nuts.

PER SERVING (½ to ⅔ cup each) **CAL** 146, **FAT** 8 g (4 g sat. fat), **CHOL** 0 mg, **SODIUM** 153 mg, **CARB** 17 g (2 g fiber, 6 g sugars), **PRO** 4 g

QUICK TIP To toast coconut, spread it in a shallow pan and bake in a 350°F oven about 5 minutes, watching closely so it doesn't burn. Toast extra and store in an airtight container in the freezer.

Tomato-Fennel
Caprese Salad

Tomato-Fennel Caprese Salad

12 g
CARB

SERVES 4
TOTAL 30 min.

- 8 asparagus spears, trimmed and cut diagonally into 2-inch pieces
- 1 small fennel bulb with fronds
- 2 cups fresh baby spinach
- 2 cups coarsely chopped or sliced assorted tomatoes
- 2 oz. fresh mozzarella cheese, cut into ¾-inch pieces
- ½ cup small fresh basil leaves
- 1 recipe Lemon-Shallot Vinaigrette
- 2 Tbsp. finely shredded Parmesan cheese

1. In a small saucepan cook asparagus in enough boiling water to cover 3 minutes; drain. Rinse with cold water to cool quickly; drain again.

2. Trim fennel bulb. Snip enough of the fennel fronds to measure 2 tsp. If desired, reserve additional fronds for garnish. Halve and core bulb; cut into very thin slices.

3. In a large bowl combine asparagus, sliced fennel, and the next four ingredients (through basil). Stir the 2 tsp. fennel fronds into Lemon-Shallot Vinaigrette. Drizzle vinaigrette over spinach mixture; toss gently to coat. Top servings with Parmesan cheese and, if desired, reserved fennel fronds.

Lemon-Shallot Vinaigrette In a small bowl whisk together ¼ cup finely chopped shallots; 3 Tbsp. lemon juice; 1 Tbsp. olive oil; 1 clove garlic, minced; and ⅛ tsp. each salt and black pepper.

Tip Use a mandoline to easily cut fennel halves into very thin slices.

PER SERVING (1½ cups each) **CAL** 129, **FAT** 7 g (2 g sat. fat), **CHOL** 12 mg, **SODIUM** 206 mg, **CARB** 12 g (4 g fiber, 6 g sugars), **PRO** 7 g

Italian Tomato-Zucchini Salad

13 g
CARB

SERVES 6
HANDS ON 30 min.
TOTAL 2 hr. 45 min.

- 12 medium roma tomatoes, sliced ⅛ inch thick
- 3 Tbsp. white wine vinegar
- 2 Tbsp. light mayonnaise
- 2 cloves garlic, minced
- ¼ tsp. salt
- ⅛ tsp. black pepper
- 4 cups long thin shreds zucchini
- ¾ cup canned no-salt-added cannellini (white kidney) beans, rinsed and drained
- 6 Tbsp. thinly sliced green onions
- ¼ cup snipped fresh basil
- 2 tsp. snipped fresh oregano or ½ tsp. dried oregano, crushed
- ¼ cup pine nuts or chopped walnuts, toasted

1. Preheat oven to 225°F. Line two baking sheets with parchment paper. Arrange tomatoes in a single layer on prepared baking sheets. Bake 1 hour. Transfer one-fourth of the tomatoes to a blender. Turn the remaining tomatoes over; bake about 75 minutes more or until dried but still slightly soft. Cool on baking sheets on wire racks.

2. For dressing, add the next five ingredients (through pepper) to tomatoes in blender. Cover and blend until smooth.

3. In a large bowl combine the next five ingredients (through oregano). Chop the dried tomatoes; add to zucchini mixture. Drizzle with dressing; toss to coat. Sprinkle servings with pine nuts. Serve immediately.

Tip To make long thin shreds, trim ends off zucchini. Slice zucchini lengthwise using a julienne peeler. Or use a vegetable spiral slicer to make zucchini "noodles." You can also cut the zucchini into long thin strips by hand or make long, thin zucchini ribbons using a vegetable peeler.

PER SERVING *(1 cup each)* **CAL** 116, **FAT** 6 g (1 g sat. fat), **CHOL** 1 mg, **SODIUM** 162 mg, **CARB** 13 g (4 g fiber, 6 g sugars), **PRO** 4 g

Orzo and Olive Salad with Spiced Citrus Vinaigrette

40 g CARB

SERVES	8
HANDS ON	35 min.
TOTAL	2 hr. 35 min.

1½ cups dried whole wheat or regular orzo pasta
½ cup orange juice
¼ cup snipped fresh mint
¼ cup lemon juice
2 Tbsp. honey
1 Tbsp. olive oil
1 tsp. ground coriander
1 tsp. grated fresh ginger
½ tsp. salt
¼ tsp. ground turmeric
¼ tsp. crushed red pepper
2 cups lightly packed fresh arugula
1 cup packaged fresh julienned carrots
¾ cup thinly sliced green onions
½ cup pitted green olives, halved
½ cup golden raisins

1. Cook orzo according to package directions; drain. Rinse with cold water; drain again.
2. Meanwhile, in a large bowl whisk together the next 10 ingredients (through crushed red pepper). Stir in orzo and the remaining ingredients. Cover and chill 2 to 24 hours.

PER SERVING (¾ cup each) **CAL** 206, **FAT** 3 g (0 g sat. fat), **CHOL** 0 mg, **SODIUM** 304 mg, **CARB** 40 g (7 g fiber, 13 g sugars), **PRO** 5 g

Sweet and Tangy
Four-Bean Salad

Sweet and Tangy Four-Bean Salad

9 g
CARB

SERVES 18
HANDS ON 30 min.
TOTAL 4 hr. 30 min.

8 oz. fresh green beans, trimmed and cut into 1-inch pieces
1 12-oz. pkg. frozen edamame
¾ cup cider vinegar
⅔ cup tomato juice
½ cup sugar
¼ cup vegetable oil
3 Tbsp. dry red wine or apple juice
2 tsp. Worcestershire sauce
2 tsp. Dijon-style mustard
1 clove garlic, minced

2 cups coarsely shredded carrots
1 15-oz. can red kidney beans, rinsed and drained
1 14.5-oz. can cut wax beans, rinsed and drained
½ cup finely chopped green onions

1. In a large saucepan cook green beans in boiling, lightly salted water 4 minutes. Stir in edamame. Cook 3 to 4 minutes more or just until tender; drain. Rinse with cold water; drain again.
2. In an extra-large bowl stir together the next eight ingredients (through

garlic). Stir in green bean mixture and the remaining ingredients. Cover and chill 4 to 48 hours.

Tip The fresh green beans will lose some color as they chill in the dressing. To retain the bright green color, cook and chill as directed, but do not add to salad. Cover and chill green bean mixture separately, then toss into salad before serving.

PER SERVING (½ cup each) **CAL** 58, **FAT** 1 g (0 g sat. fat), **CHOL** 0 mg, **SODIUM** 100 mg, **CARB** 9 g (3 g fiber, 3 g sugars), **PRO** 4 g

6

EYE-OPENING
BREAKFASTS

Get your day started right with a good balance of carbohydrate and protein to fuel your morning. Sit down to a hot and satisfying Vegetable Cheese Strata or Mexican Breakfast Pizza. If you're on the go, pair a hard-cooked egg with an Orange-Almond Breakfast Bar, Rhubarb Oat Muffin, or a Coffee Smoothie as you head out the door.

Vegetable Cheese Strata

Vegetable Cheese Strata

Vegetable Cheese Strata

24 g CARB | **SERVES** 8
HANDS ON 35 min.
TOTAL 9 hr. 35 min.

Nonstick cooking spray
5 cups cubed whole wheat
   baguette-style French bread
4 tsp. olive oil
1 cup chopped onion
1 cup chopped red sweet
   pepper
4 cloves garlic, minced
2 cups sliced fresh cremini
   mushrooms
3 cups lightly packed fresh
   spinach
1 cup shredded part-skim
   mozzarella cheese (4 oz.)
⅓ cup finely shredded Parmesan
   cheese
8 eggs
8 egg whites
1¾ cups fat-free milk
1 tablespoon Dijon-style
   mustard
½ tsp. salt
½ tsp. black pepper

1. Lightly coat a 3-qt. rectangular
baking dish with cooking spray.
Spread half of the bread cubes in
prepared dish.
2. In a 10-inch skillet heat 2 tsp. of the
oil over medium-high. Add onion,
sweet pepper, and garlic; cook until
tender, stirring occasionally. Remove
from skillet. Add remaining 2 tsp. oil to
skillet. Add mushrooms; cook and stir
until tender. Add spinach; cook until
slightly wilted. Stir in onion mixture.
3. In a small bowl stir together both
cheeses. Remove ⅓ cup of the cheese
mixture; cover and chill. Spread half of
the vegetable mixture over bread
cubes in baking dish. Sprinkle with the
remaining cheese mixture. Layer with
the remaining bread cubes and
vegetable mixture.
4. In a large bowl whisk together the
remaining ingredients. Slowly pour
over layered mixture in baking dish.
Cover and chill overnight.
5. Preheat oven to 325°F. Bake,
uncovered, 45 minutes. Sprinkle with

reserved ⅓ cup cheese mixture. Bake 5 to 10 minutes more or until a knife comes out clean. Let stand 10 minutes before serving.

PER SERVING (⅛ casserole each) **CAL** 285, **FAT** 12 g (4 g sat. fat), **CHOL** 200 mg, **SODIUM** 686 mg, **CARB** 24 g (3 g fiber, 6 g sugars), **PRO** 21 g

Sausage and Potato Casserole Cups

17 g
CARB

SERVES 6
HANDS ON 25 min.
TOTAL 55 min.

Nonstick cooking spray
8   oz. uncooked bulk Italian turkey sausage
1   medium red sweet pepper, cut into thin bite-size strips
½   cup chopped onion
3   cups frozen diced hash brown potatoes
1   Tbsp. snipped fresh oregano or 1 tsp. dried oregano, crushed
¼   tsp. black pepper
½   cup crumbled reduced-fat feta cheese or shredded Parmesan cheese (2 oz.)
5   eggs, lightly beaten
¾   cup fat-free milk

1. Preheat oven to 350°F. Coat twelve 2½-inch muffin cups with cooking spray. Coat a 10-inch skillet with cooking spray; heat over medium. Add sausage, sweet pepper, and onion; cook until sausage is browned. Add potatoes; cook 3 minutes, stirring frequently. Stir in oregano and black pepper.

2. Divide sausage mixture among prepared muffin cups (cups will be full). Top with cheese. In a bowl whisk together eggs and milk; pour over sausage mixture.

3. Bake about 25 minutes or until puffed and a knife comes out clean. Cool in cups 5 minutes. Remove from cups. If desired, top with additional cheese and fresh oregano. Serve warm.

To Store Place casserole cups in an airtight container; cover. Freeze up to 1 month. To serve each frozen cup, wrap in waxed paper and microwave about 1 minute or until heated through.

PER SERVING (2 casserole cups each) **CAL** 215, **FAT** 10 g (3 g sat. fat), **CHOL** 183 mg, **SODIUM** 438 mg, **CARB** 17 g (2 g fiber, 3 g sugars), **PRO** 16 g

Sausage and Potato Casserole Cups

Avocado Egg Chilaquiles

24g CARB

SERVES 4
HANDS ON 20 min.
TOTAL 40 min.

- 6 6-inch extra-thin corn tortillas, cut into ½-inch strips
- 1 cup lower-sodium salsa
- 1 4-oz. can diced green chile peppers, undrained
- ½ tsp. salt
- 4 eggs
- 1 cup chopped avocado
- ½ cup snipped fresh cilantro
- ¼ cup chopped red onion
   Lime wedges

1. Preheat oven to 350° F. Spread tortilla strips on a large baking sheet. Bake 10 to 12 minutes or just until starting to brown. Cool 10 minutes (strips will crisp as they cool).

2. Divide tortilla strips among four 10- to 12-oz. individual baking dishes. In a bowl stir together salsa, chile peppers, and salt; pour over tortilla strips. Bake 10 to 15 minutes or until heated through.

3. Meanwhile, coat a 12-inch nonstick skillet with *nonstick cooking spray;* heat over medium. Break eggs into skillet and cook until desired doneness.

4. Add eggs to baking dishes and sprinkle with avocado, cilantro, and onion. Serve with lime wedges.

Tip Look for a salsa with less than 100 mg sodium per 2 Tbsp.

PER SERVING *(1 individual dish each)* **CAL** 240, **FAT** 12 g (3 g sat. fat), **CHOL** 186 mg, **SODIUM** 579 mg, **CARB** 24 g (6 g fiber, 6 g sugars), **PRO** 10 g

Sausage-Egg Breakfast Burritos

28 g CARB | **SERVES** 8
HANDS ON 25 min.
TOTAL 40 min.

- 1 Tbsp. canola oil
- 2 cups finely chopped desired-color sweet peppers
- 1 cup finely chopped onion
- ½ cup fully cooked refrigerated turkey sausage crumbles
- 1 tsp. fiesta lime seasoning blend
- 4 eggs, lightly beaten
- 1 cup shredded reduced-fat cheddar cheese (4 oz.)
- 1 cup chopped, seeded tomato
- 1 Tbsp. green chile hot sauce (optional)
- 8 8-inch whole wheat or multigrain tortillas
- 1 cup fresh salsa (optional)

1. In a 10-inch nonstick skillet, heat oil over medium. Cook sweet pepper and onion in hot oil about 5 minutes or until just tender. Stir in sausage and seasoning blend.
2. Add eggs to turkey mixture in skillet. Reduce heat to medium-low. Cook until egg are setting, stirring occasionally. Remove from heat.
3. Stir cheese, tomato, and hot sauce into egg mixture. Spoon egg mixture onto tortillas just above the centers. Fold bottom edges of tortillas up and over filling. Fold in opposite sides; roll up.
4. Cut burritos in half or, to take on the go, wrap burritos halfway with foil. If desired, serve with salsa.

To Store Wrap each burrito tightly with plastic wrap. Refrigerate up to 3 days. To reheat, unwrap one burrito and rewrap with a paper towel. Microwave on 50% power (medium) 1½ to 2 minutes or until heated through. To freeze, wrap each burrito tightly with plastic wrap, then wrap with foil. Place burritos in an airtight container; cover. Freeze up to 1 month. Unwrap one frozen burrito and rewrap with a paper towel. Microwave on 30% power (medium-low) 8 to 10 minutes or until heated through, turning twice.

PER SERVING (1 burrito each) **CAL** 256, **FAT** 11 g (4 g sat. fat), **CHOL** 108 mg, **SODIUM** 494 mg, **CARB** 28 g (4 g fiber, 5 g sugars), **PRO** 13 g

Sausage-Egg Breakfast Burritos

Mexican Breakfast Pizza

Mexican Breakfast Pizza

23g CARB

SERVES 2
HANDS ON 15 min.
TOTAL 25 min.

- 2 6-inch whole wheat low-carb tortillas
- 1 egg
- 1 egg white
- 2 Tbsp. canned diced green chiles
  Nonstick cooking spray
- ¼ cup salsa
- ¼ cup canned no-salt-added black beans, drained
- 2 Tbsp. finely chopped red onion
- 2 Tbsp. finely shredded reduced-fat Mexican cheese blend
- ¼ cup chopped avocado
- 2 Tbsp. snipped fresh cilantro
- 2 lime wedges

1. Preheat oven to 400°F. Line a large baking sheet with foil or parchment paper.
2. Place tortillas directly on center oven rack. Bake about 4 minutes or just until crisp. Arrange tortillas in a single layer on prepared baking sheet.
3. In a medium bowl whisk together the egg, egg white, and chiles. Lightly coat an 8-inch nonstick skillet with cooking spray. Heat over medium. Add egg mixture and cook, without stirring, until mixture begins to set on the bottom and around edges. With a spatula, lift and fold the partially cooked egg mixture so the uncooked portion flows underneath. Continue cooking 2 to 3 minutes more or until egg mixture is cooked through but is still glossy and moist. Remove from heat.
4. Spread salsa over toasted tortillas. Top with scrambled eggs, beans, onion, and cheese. Bake 5 to 6 minutes or until heated.
5. Sprinkle pizzas with avocado and cilantro. Cut pizzas into wedges and serve warm with lime wedges.

For 4 To serve four, double the ingredients and use an extra-large baking sheet or two baking sheets.

PER SERVING (1 pizza each) **CAL** 204, **FAT** 10 g (2 g sat. fat), **CHOL** 97 mg, **SODIUM** 532 mg, **CARB** 23 g (12 g fiber, 2 g sugars), **PRO** 15 g

Spring Green Frittata

7g CARB | **SERVES** 2
TOTAL 25 min.

- 2 eggs, lightly beaten
- 4 egg whites
- 2 Tbsp. fat-free milk
- 1 tsp. snipped fresh chives
- ⅛ tsp. black pepper
- ¼ cup finely shredded Parmesan cheese (1 oz.)
- 2 tsp. olive oil
- ½ cup ½-inch pieces asparagus
- ¼ cup sliced green onions
- ½ cup coarsely chopped spinach
- 1 clove garlic, minced
- 1 small roma tomato, chopped

1. Preheat broiler. In a small bowl combine the first five ingredients (through pepper): stir in 2 Tbsp. of the cheese.

2. In an 8-inch nonstick broilerproof skillet heat oil over medium. Add asparagus and green onions; cook and stir 2 minutes. Add spinach and garlic; cook 30 seconds or just until spinach is wilted.

3. Pour egg mixture into skillet; reduce heat to low. Cook, covered, 10 to 12 minutes or until nearly set. Sprinkle with remaining 2 Tbsp. cheese.

4. Place skillet under broiler 4 to 5 inches from heat. Broil 1 minute or just until top is set and cheese is melted. Top with tomato.

PER SERVING (½ frittata each)
CAL 214, **FAT** 12 g (4 g sat. fat),
CHOL 195 mg,
SODIUM 377 mg, **CARB** 7 g
(2 g fiber, 4 g sugars),
PRO 18 g

QUICK TIP »
If mangoes are
not in season,
use thinly sliced
fresh nectarine or
peach instead.

**Mango-Bacon
Breakfast
Sandwiches**

Mango-Bacon Breakfast Sandwiches

32 g
CARB

SERVES 4
HANDS ON 20 min.
TOTAL 25 min.

8 slices lower-sodium, less-fat bacon
1 green onion
1 medium mango, halved, seeded, peeled, and thinly sliced
4 whole wheat bagel thins, split
4 ¾-oz. slices reduced-fat Monterey Jack cheese with jalapeño peppers or Colby and Monterey Jack cheese
Nonstick cooking spray

1. In a 10-inch skillet cook bacon according to package directions until crisp. Drain on paper towels. Cut bacon slices in half crosswise.
2. Thinly slice the green onion, keeping white and green parts separate; reserve the white part for another use. Top bagel thin bottoms with bacon, mango, green onion, and cheese. Add bagel thin tops.
3. Lightly coat an unheated panini press, covered indoor electric grill, or large nonstick skillet with cooking spray. Heat over medium or according to manufacturer's directions. Lightly coat outsides of sandwiches with cooking spray.
4. Place sandwiches on panini press, grill, or skillet, in batches if necessary. If using panini press or grill, close lid and grill 2 to 3 minutes or until toasted. (If using skillet, place a heavy saucepan or skillet on top of sandwiches. Cook 2 to 4 minutes or until toasted, turning once.) Serve warm.

To Make Ahead Prepare as directed through Step 2. Tightly wrap individual sandwiches with plastic wrap. Chill up to 3 days. Unwrap and continue as directed in Step 3.

PER SERVING (1 sandwich each) **CAL** 258, **FAT** 9 g (4 g sat. fat), **CHOL** 18 mg, **SODIUM** 482 mg, **CARB** 32 g (6 g fiber, 10 g sugars), **PRO** 16 g

Rhubarb Oat Muffins

Rhubarb Oat Muffins

30 g
CARB

SERVES 12
HANDS ON 20 min.
TOTAL 45 min.

Nonstick cooking spray
1¾ cups regular rolled oats
¾ cup whole wheat pastry flour or whole wheat flour
½ cup all-purpose flour
½ cup packed brown sugar*
1 tsp. baking powder
½ tsp. baking soda
¼ tsp. salt
¾ cup buttermilk
½ cup refrigerated or frozen egg product, thawed, or 2 eggs, lightly beaten
2 Tbsp. canola oil
1 tsp. vanilla
1 cup finely chopped rhubarb
1 Tbsp. packed brown sugar*
½ tsp. ground cinnamon
¼ cup chopped walnuts

1. Preheat oven to 350°F. Line twelve 2½-inch muffin cups with paper bake cups; coat paper cups with cooking spray. Or coat muffin cups with cooking spray.
2. Place ¾ cup of the oats in a food processor; cover and process until ground. Transfer to a large bowl. Stir in another ¾ cup of the oats and the next six ingredients (through salt). Make a well in center of flour mixture.
3. In a medium bowl combine the next four ingredients (through vanilla). Stir in rhubarb. Add rhubarb mixture to flour mixture; stir just until moistened (batter should be slightly lumpy). Spoon into prepared muffin cups, filling each about three-fourths full.
4. For streusel topping, in a small bowl stir together the 1 Tbsp. brown sugar and cinnamon. Stir in the remaining ¼ cup oats and the walnuts. Sprinkle over batter in muffin cups.
5. Bake 20 to 22 minutes or until a toothpick comes out clean. Cool in muffin cups on a wire rack 5 minutes. Remove from cups. Serve warm.

*Sugar Sub Choose Splenda Brown Sugar Blend. Follow package directions to use ½ cup equivalent. We do not recommend using a sugar sub in the streusel topping.

PER SERVING (1 muffin each) **CAL** 181, **FAT** 5 g (1 g sat. fat), **CHOL** 1 mg, **SODIUM** 180 mg, **CARB** 30 g (3 g fiber, 11 g sugars), **PRO** 5 g

PER SERVING WITH SUB Same as above, except **CAL** 166, **CARB** 25 g (6 g sugars)

Blueberry Muffins

24 g
CARB

SERVES 12
HANDS ON 20 min.
TOTAL 40 min.

1½ cups whole wheat flour
½ cup all-purpose flour
1½ tsp. baking powder
½ tsp. baking soda
¼ tsp. salt
2 eggs, lightly beaten
¾ cup plain yogurt or applesauce
¾ cup buttermilk, sour milk, or milk

¼ cup honey, maple syrup, or agave nectar
2 Tbsp. butter, melted, or vegetable oil
¾ cup fresh or frozen blueberries

1. Preheat oven to 400°F. Grease twelve 2½-inch muffin cups. In a medium bowl stir together the first five

ingredients (through salt). Make a well in the center of flour mixture.

2. In a bowl combine the next five ingredients (through butter). Add egg mixture all at once to flour mixture. Stir just until moistened (batter should be lumpy). Fold in blueberries. Spoon batter into the prepared muffin cups, filling each half to two-thirds full.

3. Bake 15 to 18 minutes or until golden. Cool in muffin cups on a wire rack 5 minutes. Remove from muffin cups; serve warm.

Tip To make ¾ cup sour milk, place 2 tsp. lemon juice or vinegar in a glass measuring cup. Add enough milk to make ¾ cup total liquid; stir. Let stand 5 minutes before using.

PER SERVING (*1 muffin each*) **CAL** 144, **FAT** 4 g (2 g sat. fat), **CHOL** 38 mg, **SODIUM** 216 mg, **CARB** 24 g (2 g fiber, 9 g sugars), **PRO** 5 g

Overnight Chia-Almond Pancakes with Berry Syrup

37g
CARB

SERVES 8
HANDS ON 20 min.
TOTAL 30 min.

- 1¼ cups white whole wheat flour
- 1 cup all-purpose flour
- 2 Tbsp. chia seeds, ground
- 1 Tbsp. sugar*
- 1 Tbsp. baking powder
- ½ tsp. salt
- 2¼ cups unsweetened original soymilk
- 2 eggs, lightly beaten
- ¼ cup canola oil
- ½ tsp. almond extract
- 1 recipe Berry Syrup
- ¼ cup slivered almonds, toasted

1. In a large bowl stir together the first six ingredients (through salt). In another bowl combine soymilk, eggs, oil, and almond extract. Cover and chill bowls separately up to 24 hours.

2. To make pancakes, add soymilk mixture all at once to flour mixture. Stir just until moistened (batter should be slightly lumpy).

3. For each pancake, pour about ¼ cup batter onto a hot, lightly greased griddle or heavy skillet; spread batter. (If batter is too thick, thin with a little additional soymilk.) Cook over medium 3 to 4 minutes per side or until pancakes are lightly golden. Turn over when surfaces are bubbly and edges are slightly dry.

4. To serve, drizzle pancakes with Berry Syrup and sprinkle with almonds.

Berry Syrup In a small saucepan melt **⅓ cup low-sugar orange strawberry preserves** over medium-low. In a bowl whisk together **⅓ cup orange juice** and **½ tsp. cornstarch** until smooth; add to preserves. Cook and stir over medium-low until thickened and bubbly. Cook and stir 1 minute more. Stir in **½ cup chopped strawberries.**

To Freeze Layer cooked pancakes between sheets of wax paper. Place in an airtight container; cover. Freeze up to 1 month. To reheat, microwave one frozen pancake wrapped in waxed paper 30 to 40 seconds or until heated (or remove from waxed paper and toast frozen pancake in a toaster 2 to 3 minutes or until heated).

***Sugar Sub** Choose Splenda Sugar Blend. Follow package directions for 1 Tbsp. equivalent.

PER SERVING (2 pancakes + 2 Tbsp. syrup + 1½ tsp. almonds each) **CAL** 287, **FAT** 12 g (1 g sat. fat), **CHOL** 47 mg, **SODIUM** 370 mg, **CARB** 37 g (4 g fiber, 7 g sugars), **PRO** 9 g

PER SERVING WITH SUB Same as above, except **CAL** 285, **CARB** 36 g (6 g sugars)

Overnight Chia-Almond Pancakes with Berry Syrup

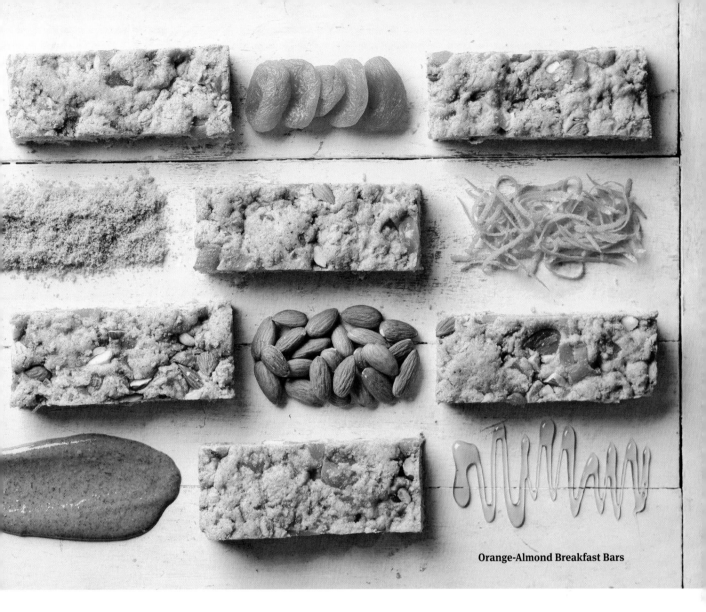

Orange-Almond Breakfast Bars

Orange-Almond Breakfast Bars

35 g
CARB

SERVES 16
HANDS ON 20 min.
TOTAL 35 min.

Nonstick cooking spray
1 large orange
¼ cup packed brown sugar*
1 cup chopped pitted whole dried dates and/or dried apricots
1¼ cups all-purpose flour
1¼ cups whole wheat flour
½ tsp. baking soda
¼ tsp. baking powder
¼ tsp. salt
1 egg, lightly beaten
⅓ cup honey
¼ cup almond butter
1 cup chopped almonds

1. Preheat oven to 350°F. Line a 13×9-inch baking pan with foil, extending foil over the edges of pan. Lightly coat foil with cooking spray.
2. Remove 1 tsp. zest and squeeze ½ cup orange juice from orange. In a bowl combine zest, juice, and brown sugar. Stir in dates and/or apricots. In a large bowl stir together the next five ingredients (through salt).
3. Whisk egg, honey, and almond butter into fruit mixture. Add egg mixture and almonds to flour mixture. Stir until moistened. Spoon into the prepared baking pan. Use moistened hands to pat dough evenly in pan.
4. Bake about 12 minutes or until edges are brown and a toothpick comes out clean. Cool in pan on a wire rack. Cut into bars.

To Store Layer bars between sheets of waxed paper in an airtight container; cover. Store at room temperature up to 2 days or freeze up to 3 months.

*Sugar Sub Choose Splenda Brown Sugar Blend. Follow package directions to use ¼ cup equivalent.

PER SERVING (1 bar each) **CAL** 205, **FAT** 6 g (1 g sat. fat), **CHOL** 12 mg, **SODIUM** 99 mg, **CARB** 35 g (3 g fiber, 17 g sugars), **PRO** 5 g

PER SERVING WITH SUB Same as above, except **CAL** 200, **CARB** 33 g (16 g sugars)

QUICK TIP Before scooping the dough to drop onto cookie sheets, lightly coat the $\frac{1}{4}$-cup measure with nonstick cooking spray so the dough slips out easily.

Banana-Oat Breakfast Cookies

Banana-Oat Breakfast Cookies

34 g
CARB

SERVES	12
HANDS ON	20 min.
TOTAL	35 min.

- ½ cup mashed banana
- ½ cup chunky peanut butter or almond butter
- ½ cup honey
- 2 Tbsp. fat-free milk or almond milk
- 1 tsp. vanilla
- 1 cup regular or quick-cooking rolled oats
- ½ cup whole wheat flour
- 2 tsp. ground cinnamon
- ¼ tsp. baking soda
- 1 cup dried cranberries, cherries, apples, or raisins

1. Preheat oven to 350°F. Line two cookie sheets with parchment paper. In a large bowl stir together the first five ingredients (through vanilla). In a small bowl stir together oats, flour, cinnamon, and baking soda. Stir oat mixture into banana mixture until combined. Stir in dried cranberries.

2. Using a ¼-cup measure, drop dough in mounds 3 inches apart onto the prepared cookie sheets. Using a narrow metal or small plastic spatula dipped in water, flatten and spread the mounds to 2¾-inch diameter (about ½ inch thick).

3. Bake 14 to 16 minutes or until cookies are brown. Remove; cool cookies on wire rack.

To Store Layer cookies between sheets of waxed paper in an airtight container; cover. Store in the refrigerator up to 3 days or freeze up to 2 months.

PER SERVING *(1 cookie each)* **CAL** 193, **FAT** 6 g (1 g sat. fat), **CHOL** 0 mg, **SODIUM** 80 mg, **CARB** 34 g (3 g fiber, 21 g sugars), **PRO** 4 g

Quick Skillet Granola with Fruit and Yogurt

Quick Skillet Granola with Fruit and Yogurt

41 g
CARB

SERVES	4
TOTAL	20 min.

- ⅔ cup regular rolled oats
- ⅓ cup slivered almonds
- 2 Tbsp. flaxseeds
- 2 Tbsp. light butter
- 1 Tbsp. honey
- ½ tsp. ground cinnamon
- 2 medium bananas, peeled and sliced crosswise
- 1 cup fresh strawberries, hulled and quartered
- 2 5.3- to 6-oz. cartons fruit-flavored light Greek yogurt

1. Heat a 10-inch nonstick skillet over medium. Add oats and almonds. Cook, stirring frequently, 3 to 5 minutes or until mixture is lightly browned. (Reduce heat to medium-low if mixture browns too quickly.) Stir in flaxseeds, butter, honey, and cinnamon. Cook and stir 1 to 2 minutes more or until most of the liquid is absorbed and the almonds and oats are golden brown. Remove from heat.

2. Serve granola with bananas, strawberries, and yogurt.

PER SERVING *(⅓ cup granola + ⅔ cup fruit + ⅓ cup yogurt each)* **CAL** 281, **FAT** 10 g (2 g sat. fat), **CHOL** 10 mg, **SODIUM** 84 mg, **CARB** 41 g (9 g fiber, 18 g sugars), **PRO** 11 g

Fruity Coconut Smoothie Bowls with Toasted Oats

33 g
CARB

SERVES 4
TOTAL 20 min.

⅓ cup regular rolled oats
⅓ cup unsweetened coconut flakes
1½ cups refrigerated unsweetened coconut milk beverage
1 cup unsweetened frozen mango chunks
1 cup unsweetened frozen raspberries
1 cup unsweetened frozen blueberries
½ cup peeled and seeded chopped fresh mango
½ cup fresh raspberries
½ cup fresh blueberries
½ cup slivered almonds, toasted

1. Heat an 8-inch skillet over medium. Add oats and coconut. Cook, stirring frequently, 3 to 5 minutes or until oats and coconut are lightly toasted. Remove from heat.

2. Meanwhile, in a blender combine coconut milk, frozen mango, frozen raspberries, and frozen blueberries. Cover; blend until smooth, stopping and scraping container as needed.

3. To serve, pour smoothie into four shallow bowls. Top with toasted oats and coconut and the remaining ingredients.

PER SERVING *(1½ cups each)* **CAL** 252, **FAT** 13 g (5 g sat. fat), **CHOL** 0 mg, **SODIUM** 18 mg, **CARB** 33 g (8 g fiber, 18 g sugars), **PRO** 5 g

Coffee Smoothies

Cherry-Berry
Oatmeal
Smoothies

Coffee Smoothies

28 g
CARB

SERVES 8
TOTAL 15 min.

- ⅓ cup hot water
- 2 Tbsp. instant espresso coffee powder
- 3 cups cut-up bananas (4 large), frozen
- 1½ cups fat-free milk
- ⅓ cup honey
- 3 cups ice cubes
  Ground cinnamon (optional)

1. In a blender, in batches if necessary, combine the hot water and espresso powder; let stand 1 minute. Add frozen bananas, milk, and honey. Cover and blend until smooth. Add ice cubes. Cover and blend until nearly smooth. If desired, sprinkle servings lightly with cinnamon.

PER SERVING (⅔ cup each) **CAL** 113, **FAT** 0 g, **CHOL** 1 mg, **SODIUM** 21 mg, **CARB** 28 g (1 g fiber, 21 g sugars), **PRO** 2 g

Cherry-Berry Oatmeal Smoothies

21 g
CARB

SERVES 3
HANDS ON 10 min.
TOTAL 15 min.

- ½ cup water
- ⅓ cup quick-cooking rolled oats
- ½ cup light almond milk or fat-free milk
- ¾ cup fresh or frozen unsweetened strawberries, partially thawed
- ½ cup fresh or frozen unsweetened pitted dark sweet cherries, partially thawed
- 1 to 2 Tbsp. almond butter
- 1 Tbsp. honey
- ½ cup small ice cubes

1. In a medium bowl combine water and oats. Microwave 1 minute. Stir in ¼ cup of the milk. Microwave 30 to 50 seconds more or until oats are very tender. Cool 5 minutes.

2. In a blender combine oat mixture, the remaining ¼ cup milk, and the next four ingredients (through honey). Cover and blend until smooth, scraping container as needed. Add ice cubes; cover and blend until smooth. If desired, top each serving with additional fruit.

For 6 This recipe easily doubles to make 6 servings. If necessary, blend in batches.

PER SERVING (¾ cup each) **CAL** 121, **FAT** 4 g (0 g sat. fat), **CHOL** 0 mg, **SODIUM** 41 mg, **CARB** 21 g (3 g fiber, 12 g sugars), **PRO** 3 g

GOOD-FOR-YOU
SNACKS

Snacks between meals should keep you going without a big sugar

hit. Enjoy refreshing Fresh-Squeezed Pink Lemonade Pops after

a hot-day walk, protein-filled Banana Energy Bites to power you

through a midafternoon munchie attack, and 7-Layer Fruit Dip for

a pick-me-up with friends.

Fresh-Squeezed
Pink Lemonade
Ice Pops

Fresh-Squeezed Pink Lemonade Ice Pops

11 g
CARB

SERVES 7
HANDS ON 15 min.
TOTAL 8 hr. 15 min.

1¾ cups water
¾ cup lemon juice
⅓ cup sugar*
   Red food coloring
   Snipped fresh basil or small fresh basil leaves (optional)

1. In a 4-cup liquid measure combine the water, lemon juice, and sugar, stirring until sugar is dissolved. Tint with food coloring. If desired, add basil (it will float on top initially).
2. Pour mixture into seven 3-oz. paper cups or ice pop molds. Insert sticks in molds. If using paper cups, cover each cup with foil. Cut a small slit in foil and insert a wooden stick into each cup. Freeze 1½ hours, gently shaking molds or stirring mixture in cups to disperse basil. Freeze overnight or until firm.

*Sugar Sub We do not recommend a sugar sub for this recipe.

PER SERVING *(1 ice pop each)* **CAL** 43, **FAT** 0 g, **CHOL** 0 mg, **SODIUM** 2 mg, **CARB** 11 g (0 g fiber, 10 g sugars), **PRO** 0 g

» QUICK TIP
Be sure to use foil bake cups to line muffin cups. Paper liners get soggy and tear easily.

Strawberry-Banana FroYo Cups

Strawberry-Banana FroYo Cups

11 g
CARB

SERVES 12
HANDS ON 15 min.
TOTAL 4 hr. 15 min.

3 overripe bananas, peeled
2 cups strawberry fat-free Greek yogurt
½ cup chopped strawberries

1. Line twelve 2½-inch muffin cups with foil bake cups. In a large bowl mash bananas with a fork until smooth. Stir in yogurt. Spoon into the prepared muffin cups. Top with chopped strawberries. Cover and freeze 4 to 5 hours or until firm. If necessary, let stand at room temperature 10 minutes to soften before eating.

PER SERVING *(1 frozen dessert each)*
CAL 62, **FAT** 1 g (1 g sat. fat), **CHOL** 4 mg, **SODIUM** 11 mg, **CARB** 11 g (1 g fiber, 8 g sugars), **PRO** 3 g

Walnut Butter Fruit Bites

7g CARB | **SERVES** 64
TOTAL 20 min.

- 8 Medjool dates, pitted
- 1 cup snipped dried apricots
- 4 cups whole grain wheat cereal flakes
- 1½ cups Walnut-Maple Butter or cashew butter
- 1 cup walnut or cashew pieces

1. Place dates and apricots in a food processor. Cover and pulse until very finely chopped. Add cereal; pulse until cereal is chopped. Add Walnut-Maple Butter; process until combined and mixture holds together.

2. Line an 8-inch square baking pan with foil, extending foil over edges of pan. Press mixture firmly into pan. Sprinkle nuts on top; press firmly to adhere. Using the edges of the foil, lift uncut bars out of pan; cut into 1-inch squares.

Walnut-Maple Butter Place **3 cups walnut halves, toasted,** in a food processor. Cover and process until finely chopped. Add **3 Tbsp. pure maple syrup, ⅛ tsp. salt,** and a **dash ground cinnamon.** Cover and process about 5 minutes more or until nearly smooth, stopping and scraping down sides of bowl as needed. Cover and chill about 1 hour. Makes 1⅓ cups.

To Store Layer bites between sheets of waxed paper in an airtight container; cover. Store in the refrigerator up to 1 week.

PER SERVING (1 bite each) **CAL** 71, **FAT** 5 g (0 g sat. fat), **CHOL** 0 mg, **SODIUM** 21 mg, **CARB** 7 g (1 g fiber, 4 g sugars), **PRO** 1 g

Banana Energy Bites

14g CARB | **SERVES** 16
TOTAL 30 min.

- 1 overripe banana, peeled
- 1 cup uncooked quick-cooking rolled oats
- ½ cup roasted and salted pumpkin seeds (pepitas)
- ½ cup dried cranberries
- ½ cup natural peanut butter
- ¼ cup miniature semisweet chocolate pieces

1. In a medium bowl mash banana with a fork until smooth. Stir in the remaining ingredients. Using 1 Tbsp. for each bite, shape into 32 balls; flatten slightly. Chill until ready to serve.

To Store Layer bites between sheets of waxed paper in an airtight container. Store in refrigerator up to 3 days or freeze up to 3 months.

PER SERVING (2 bites each) **CAL** 145, **FAT** 9 g (2 g sat. fat), **CHOL** 0 mg, **SODIUM** 53 mg, **CARB** 14 g (2 g fiber, 7 g sugars), **PRO** 5 g

Walnut Butter Fruit Bites

Banana Energy Bites

QUICK TIP Roast chickpeas as long as you can before overbrowning so they get as crisp as possible. You can also recrisp stored chickpeas in a 350°F oven 5 minutes.

Barbecue-Spiced
Roasted Chickpeas

Barbecue-Spiced Roasted Chickpeas

10 g
CARB

SERVES 12
HANDS ON 5 min.
TOTAL 40 min.

- 2 15-oz. cans no-salt-added chickpeas (garbanzo beans), rinsed and drained
- ¼ cup olive oil
- 1 tsp. barbecue spice
- 1 tsp. paprika
- 1 tsp. chili powder
- ¼ tsp. garlic salt
- ¼ tsp. celery salt
- ¼ tsp. onion powder

1. Preheat oven to 450°F. In a bowl combine all ingredients; stir to coat. In a 15×10-inch baking pan spread chickpeas in an even layer. Roast about 30 minutes or until browned and crisp, stirring once halfway through roasting. Cool completely.

To Store Place cooled chickpeas in an airtight container; cover. Store at room temperature up to 1 week.

PER SERVING (¼ cup each) **CAL** 101, **FAT** 5 g (1 g sat. fat), **CHOL** 0 mg, **SODIUM** 122 mg, **CARB** 10 g (3 g fiber, 0 g sugars), **PRO** 4 g

Creamy Avocado-Horseradish Dip

Creamy Avocado-Horseradish Dip

6 g
CARB

SERVES 6
TOTAL 15 min.

- 1 medium ripe avocado, halved, seeded, and peeled
- ¼ cup light mayonnaise
- 2 Tbsp. finely chopped green onion
- 2 tsp. lemon juice
- 1 to 2 tsp. prepared horseradish
- ⅛ tsp. salt
- 1 head Belgian endive
- 2 cups carrot sticks, sweet pepper strips, and/or broccoli florets

1. In a medium bowl finely mash avocado using a fork. Stir in the next five ingredients (through salt) until well combined.
2. Trim endive. Separate into leaves. Serve dip with endive leaves and carrot sticks, pepper strips, and/or broccoli florets.

To Make Ahead Prepare as directed in Step 1. Cover surface of dip completely with plastic wrap. Chill up to 8 hours.

PER SERVING (2 Tbsp. dip + 2 leaves endive + ⅓ cup other vegetables each) **CAL** 87, **FAT** 7 g (1 g sat. fat), **CHOL** 4 mg, **SODIUM** 131 mg, **CARB** 6 g (3 g fiber, 2 g sugars), **PRO** 1 g

Beet Hummus

15 g CARB

SERVES 10
HANDS ON 15 min.
TOTAL 40 min.

1 lb. fresh beets with tops, trimmed, peeled, and cut into chunks
1 15-oz. can reduced-sodium garbanzo beans (chickpeas), rinsed and drained
3 Tbsp. tahini (sesame seed paste)
3 Tbsp. lemon juice
2 cloves garlic, minced
½ tsp. salt
3 Tbsp. canola oil
2 Tbsp. plain fat-free Greek yogurt
Cucumber slices and/or carrot or celery sticks

1. In a covered large saucepan cook beets in enough boiling water to cover about 25 minutes or until tender; drain and cool slightly.

2. In a food processor combine beets and the next five ingredients (through salt). Cover and process until nearly smooth. With processor running, slowly add oil in a steady stream until combined.

3. Transfer hummus to a bowl. Swirl in yogurt. Serve with cucumber slices and/or carrot or celery sticks as dippers.

PER SERVING (¼ cup hummus each)
CAL 131, **FAT** 7 g (1 g sat. fat), **CHOL** 0 mg, **SODIUM** 250 mg, **CARB** 15 g (4 g fiber, 4 g sugars), **PRO** 4 g

Tomato-Lentil Salsa with Cumin-Spiced Chips

19 g CARB

SERVES 6
HANDS ON 20 min.
TOTAL 8 hr. 20 min.

1 large tomato, cored and chopped
½ cup refrigerated cooked lentils
¼ cup chopped fresh mango
¼ cup finely chopped radishes
¼ cup thinly sliced green onions
1 small fresh serrano chile pepper, seeded if desired and finely chopped (tip, *p. 154*)
1 Tbsp. snipped fresh cilantro
1 Tbsp. snipped fresh mint
1 Tbsp. lemon juice
1 recipe Cumin-Spiced Chips

1. In a bowl stir together the first nine ingredients (through lemon juice). Cover and chill up to 8 hours. Serve with Cumin-Spiced Chips.

Cumin-Spiced Chips Preheat oven to 375°F. Lightly coat a large baking sheet with **nonstick cooking spray.** Place **4 oz. plain pita chips** in a large bowl. Lightly coat chips with the **cooking spray.** In a small bowl stir together **1 tsp. paprika, ½ tsp. garlic powder, ¼ tsp. each ground coriander and ground cumin,** and a **pinch salt.** Sprinkle chips with spices while tossing gently to coat. Spread chips in a single layer on prepared baking sheet. Bake 4 to 5 minutes or until lightly browned.

PER SERVING (⅓ *cup salsa + ¾ oz. chips each*) **CAL** 123, **FAT** 4 g (0 g sat. fat), **CHOL** 0 mg, **SODIUM** 247 mg, **CARB** 19 g (3 g fiber, 3 g sugars), **PRO** 4 g

Tomato-Lentil Salsa with Cumin-Spiced Chips

Ham-Wrapped Stuffed Celery Sticks

7-Layer Fruit Dip

17g
CARB

SERVES 8
TOTAL 15 min.

- ½ of an 8-oz. pkg. reduced-fat cream cheese (neufchatel), softened
- 1 Tbsp. honey
- ¼ tsp. ground cinnamon
- ¼ tsp. ground ginger
- ⅓ cup plain fat-free Greek-style yogurt
- 3 small clementines, peeled and divided into segments
- 2 Tbsp. snipped pitted dates or golden raisins
- 2 Tbsp. unsweetened shredded coconut, toasted
- 2 Tbsp. chopped dry-roasted salted pistachio nuts
- 2 Tbsp. snipped fresh mint
- 48 almond nut thins

1. In a bowl stir together cream cheese, honey, cinnamon, and ginger until well combined. Spread mixture into an 8-inch-diameter circle on a serving plate. Spread yogurt evenly over cream cheese mixture, leaving about a ½-inch border around the edge. Arrange orange segments in a single layer on the yogurt.
2. Sprinkle dates, coconut, pistachio nuts, and mint over orange segments. Serve immediately or cover and chill dip up to 12 hours. Serve with nut thins for scooping.

PER SERVING (2 Tbsp. dip + 6 nut thins each) **CAL** 133, **FAT** 6 g (2 g sat. fat), **CHOL** 10 mg, **SODIUM** 104 mg, **CARB** 17 g (1 g fiber, 7 g sugars), **PRO** 4 g

Ham-Wrapped Stuffed Celery Sticks

5g
CARB

SERVES 6
TOTAL 15 min.

- 3 oz. goat cheese (chèvre), softened
- ¼ cup light cream cheese spread, softened
- 1 Tbsp. snipped fresh chives
- 1 Tbsp. honey
- ¼ tsp. freshly ground black pepper
- 6 stalks celery
- 1½ oz. thinly sliced lower-sodium ham

1. In a bowl stir together the first five ingredients (through pepper) until well combined.
2. Trim celery stalks. Cut stalks in half crosswise. Spread cheese mixture evenly into celery sticks. Cut ham slices lengthwise into 12 strips total. Wrap strips around the centers of celery sticks.

PER SERVING (2 sticks each) **CAL** 104, **FAT** 7 g (4 g sat. fat), **CHOL** 22 mg, **SODIUM** 221 mg, **CARB** 5 g (1 g fiber, 4 g sugars), **PRO** 6 g

DELIGHTFUL
DESSERTS

You too, deserve something sweet. These carb-conscious desserts

are filled with mindful ingredients. Frozen Neapolitans and Frozen

Yogurt Bark will make the freezer your ally, keeping temptation

on ice so you can sample a little at a time. All these delicious,

satisfying desserts have just-right serving sizes.

Strawberry Swirl Cheesecake Ice Pops

Strawberry Swirl Cheesecake Ice Pops

16 g CARB

SERVES 8
HANDS ON 30 min.
TOTAL 8 hr. 30 min.

- 1 cup chopped fresh or frozen strawberries, thawed
- 2 Tbsp. sugar*
- 1 4-serving-size pkg. fat-free, sugar-free, reduced-calorie cheesecake instant pudding mix
- 2 cups fat-free milk
- 1 cup frozen light whipped topping, thawed
- ⅓ cup crushed graham crackers
- 1 Tbsp. butter, melted

1. In a food processor or blender combine strawberries and sugar. Cover and process or blend until smooth. In a medium bowl whisk together pudding mix and milk 2 to 3 minutes or until thick. Fold in whipped topping.

2. Spoon pudding mixture into eight 5-ounce paper cups or ice-pop molds. Top with pureed strawberries; swirl slightly to marble. In a small bowl combine graham crackers and melted butter. Top strawberry layer with crumb mixture.

3. Cover each cup with foil. Cut a small slit in foil and insert a wooden stick into each pop. If using molds, insert sticks into molds. Freeze overnight or until firm.

*****Sugar Sub** Choose Splenda Sugar Blend. Follow package directions to use 2 Tbsp. equivalent.

PER SERVING *(1 ice pop each)* **CAL** 99, **FAT** 3 g (2 g sat. fat), **CHOL** 5 mg, **SODIUM** 197 mg, **CARB** 16 g (0 g fiber, 9 g sugars), **PRO** 2 g

PER SERVING WITH SUB Same as above, except **CAL** 95, **CARB** 15 g (7 g sugars)

Citus Custard

28 g **CARB**

SERVES 4
HANDS ON 30 min.
TOTAL 4 hr. 30 min.

- ¼ **cup sugar***
- 2 **Tbsp. cornstarch**
- 2½ **cups low-fat (1%) milk**
- 4 **egg yolks, lightly beaten**
- ½ **tsp. orange zest**
- ½ **tsp. vanilla**
- ¼ **cup coarsely crushed shortbread cookies**
  Orange slices and/or citrus peel twists (optional)

1. In a medium heavy saucepan stir together sugar and cornstarch; stir in milk. Cook and stir over medium until thick and bubbly. Cook and stir 2 minutes more. Remove from heat.

2. Gradually stir about 1 cup of the hot mixture into egg yolks; return to the remaining hot mixture in saucepan. Bring just to boiling; remove from heat. Stir in orange zest and vanilla. Pour into a serving bowl or dessert bowls and cover surface with plastic wrap; cool slightly. Chill at least 4 hours before serving; do not stir.

3. Top custard with crushed cookies and, if desired, orange slices and/or twists.

***Sugar Sub** We do not recommend a sugar sub for this recipe.

PER SERVING (⅔ cup each) **CAL** 212, **FAT** 7 g (3 g sat. fat), **CHOL** 192 mg, **SODIUM** 95 mg, **CARB** 28 g (0 g fiber, 22 g sugars), **PRO** 8 g

Frozen Neapolitans

Frozen Neapolitans

18 g
CARB

SERVES 24
HANDS ON 25 min.
TOTAL 5 hr. 35 min.

- 4 cups chocolate-flavor crisp rice cereal
- 1¼ cups chopped toasted almonds
- 2 Tbsp. butter
- 2 cups tiny marshmallows
- 1 pint chocolate ice cream
- 1 pint vanilla ice cream
- 1 pint strawberry ice cream
- ½ cup miniature semisweet chocolate pieces or ⅓ cup chocolate-flavor syrup ice cream topping (optional)

1. Line a 13×9-inch baking pan with foil, extending foil over edges of pan. Butter foil. In a bowl combine cereal and ¾ cup of the almonds.
2. In a large saucepan melt butter over low. Add marshmallows; heat and stir until melted. Remove from heat. Add cereal mixture; stir gently to coat. Using a buttered rubber scraper, press mixture firmly into the prepared pan. Freeze 10 minutes.
3. Let ice creams stand at room temperature 5 minutes to soften before spreading. Spread chocolate ice cream evenly over cereal layer. Freeze about 30 minutes or until firm. Spread vanilla ice cream over chocolate ice cream; freeze about 30 minutes or until firm. Spread strawberry ice cream over vanilla ice cream. Sprinkle with remaining ½ cup almonds. If desired, sprinkle with chocolate pieces or drizzle with chocolate syrup. Cover and freeze about 4 hours or until firm.
4. Use foil to lift frozen mixture out of pan. Cut into about 1½-inch squares. Let stand 10 minutes before serving.

To Make Ahead Place squares in a single layer in an airtight container; cover. Store in the freezer up to 1 month.

PER SERVING *(2 bars each)* CAL 142, FAT 6 g (4 g sat. fat), CHOL 14 mg, SODIUM 72 mg, CARB 18 g (2 g fiber, 12 g sugars), PRO 2 g

Banana Split Sundaes

27 g
CARB

SERVES 4
HANDS ON 10 min.
TOTAL 2 hr. 10 min.

- 3 overripe bananas, sliced and frozen
- 2 Tbsp. peanut butter
- ¼ cup frozen light whipped topping, thawed
- 2 Tbsp. sugar-free chocolate-flavor syrup
- 4 tsp. chopped peanuts
- 4 maraschino cherries

1. In a food processor combine bananas and peanut butter. Cover and process until nearly smooth. Scoop into sundae dishes. Top with remaining ingredients. Serve immediately.

Tip To freeze bananas, peel and slice very ripe bananas, then arrange in a single layer on a large plate. Freeze at least 2 hours or until firm.

PER SERVING *(⅓ cup each)* CAL 166, FAT 6 g (2 g sat. fat), CHOL 0 mg, SODIUM 60 mg, CARB 27 g (3 g fiber, 14 g sugars), PRO 3 g

Banana Split Sundaes

Frozen Yogurt Bark

9g CARB

SERVES 24
HANDS ON 15 min.
TOTAL 2 hr. 15 min.

- 1 32-oz. carton plain whole-milk Greek yogurt
- ¼ cup honey or 2 tbsp. agave syrup
- 2 tsp. vanilla or 1 tsp. almond extract
- 1 cup filling(s), such as chopped dark chocolate, berries, and/or nuts
- 2 cups topper(s), such as toasted raw chip coconut, nuts, or seeds; fruit; and/or cacao nibs

1. Line two large baking sheets or trays with parchment paper. In a large bowl combine yogurt, honey, and vanilla. Stir in filling(s).
2. Divide yogurt mixture between prepared baking sheets, spreading into rectangles. Sprinkle with topper(s).
3. Freeze 2 to 4 hours or until firm. To serve, break bark into 24 irregular pieces. Store in freezer.

PER SERVING (1 piece each) **CAL** 117, **FAT** 7 g (4 g sat. fat), **CHOL** 5 mg, **SODIUM** 14 mg, **CARB** 9 g (2 g fiber, 6 g sugars), **PRO** 5 g

Creamy Mango Soft Serve

Creamy Mango Soft Serve

29g CARB

SERVES 2
TOTAL 10 min.

- 1 cup chopped frozen mango
- ½ cup no-sugar-added or low-sugar vanilla ice cream
- 3 Tbsp. lite coconut milk
- 1 tsp. sugar*
- 1 tsp. lime juice
- ½ tsp. vanilla
- ¼ cup chopped fresh mango

1. In a food processor combine first six ingredients (through vanilla) in the order listed. Process until smooth. Serve immediately or freeze 1 hour to firm slightly. Top servings with the chopped mango.

*Sugar Sub We do not recommend a sugar sub for this recipe.

PER SERVING (¾ cup each) **CAL** 151, **FAT** 4 g (3 g sat. fat), **CHOL** 18 mg, **SODIUM** 34 mg, **CARB** 29 g (1 g fiber, 22 g sugars), **PRO** 2 g

« **QUICK TIP** Whole-milk yogurt may have a touch more fat. The fat helps to make a creamy-melting bark that isn't icy.

Frozen Yogurt Bark

Raspberry-Chocolate-Almond Ice Cream

Raspberry-Chocolate Almond Ice Cream

18 g
CARB

SERVES 8
HANDS ON 20 min.
TOTAL 12 hr. 20 min.

- 2 cups unsweetened vanilla-flavored almond milk
- 3 egg yolks
- ¼ cup honey
- 2 Tbsp. cornstarch
- ¼ tsp. almond extract
- ⅛ tsp. salt
- 1 cup fresh raspberries
- 2 oz. dark chocolate, finely chopped
- ⅓ cup slivered almonds, toasted

1. In a medium saucepan whisk together the first four ingredients (through cornstarch). Cook and stir over medium 6 to 8 minutes or until mixture coats the back of a spoon. (Do not boil.) If necessary to remove any lumps, strain through a fine-mesh sieve into a bowl; stir in almond extract and salt. Cover and chill 8 to 24 hours.

2. Pour chilled mixture into a 1½-qt. ice cream freezer. Freeze according to the manufacturer's directions. Stir in the remaining ingredients. Transfer mixture to a 2-qt. freezer container. Cover and freeze 4 hours before serving.

PER SERVING (½ cup each) CAL 142, FAT 7 g (2 g sat. fat), CHOL 70 mg, SODIUM 87 mg, CARB 18 g (2 g fiber, 13 g sugars), PRO 3 g

Chocolate-Caramel-Peanut Crunch Pie

23 g
CARB

SERVES 10
HANDS ON 25 min.
TOTAL 2 hr. 40 min.

- Nonstick cooking spray
- 2 Tbsp. butter, softened
- 2 Tbsp. creamy peanut butter
- ¼ cup packed brown sugar*
- 1 egg white
- ½ tsp. vanilla
- ⅓ cup all-purpose flour
- ½ cup quick-cooking rolled oats
- ⅓ cup finely crushed graham crackers
- 1 4-serving-size pkg. sugar-free, low-calorie instant chocolate pudding mix
- 1½ cups fat-free milk
- ¾ cup frozen light whipped dessert topping, thawed
- ¼ cup unsalted dry-roasted peanuts, coarsely chopped
- 1 Tbsp. sugar-free caramel-flavored ice cream topping

1. Preheat oven to 350°F. Generously coat a 9-inch pie plate with cooking spray. In a bowl beat butter and peanut butter with a mixer on medium to high 30 seconds. Add brown sugar. Beat until combined, scraping bowl occasionally. Beat in egg white and vanilla until combined. Beat in flour. Stir in oats and finely crushed graham crackers.

2. Using damp fingers, press oat mixture onto bottom and up sides of the prepared pie plate, pressing mixture slightly up onto edge of pie plate. Coat one side of a double layer of foil with cooking spray. Line crust with foil, cooking spray side down. Bake 8 minutes. Carefully remove foil. Bake 5 to 7 minutes more or until crust is lightly browned. Cool completely on a wire rack.

3. In a medium bowl whisk together pudding mix and milk 2 minutes. Pour into cooled crust. Chill 1 hour. Spread dessert topping over pudding layer. Cover loosely. Chill 1 to 24 hours before serving. Before serving, sprinkle with peanuts and drizzle with ice cream topping.

*Sugar Sub We do not recommend a sugar sub for this recipe.

PER SERVING (1 wedge each) CAL 166, FAT 7 g (3 g sat. fat), CHOL 7 mg, SODIUM 195 mg, CARB 23 g (1 g fiber, 9 g sugars), PRO 5 g

Chocolate-Caramel-
Peanut Crunch Pie

Creamy Chocolate Pudding

Creamy Chocolate Pudding

26 g
CARB

| **SERVES** 4 |
| **TOTAL** 10 min. |

1 ripe avocado, halved, seeded, peeled, and cut up
½ of a banana, cut up
½ cup milk or soymilk
½ cup unsweetened cocoa powder
3 to 4 Tbsp. honey or agave
2 tsp. vanilla

1. In a blender combine all of the ingredients. Cover and blend until smooth. If desired, cover surface with plastic wrap and chill before serving.

2. If desired, sprinkle with additional unsweetened cocoa powder.

PER SERVING (about ½ cup each)
CAL 163, FAT 7 g (2 g sat. fat), CHOL 2 mg, SODIUM 20 mg, CARB 26 g (6 g fiber, 14 g sugars), PRO 4 g

Apple-Maple Snack Cake

15 g
CARB

SERVES 16	
HANDS ON 15 min.	
TOTAL 35 min.	

Nonstick cooking spray
1 cup white whole wheat flour
1 tsp. baking powder
¾ tsp. apple pie spice
¼ tsp. salt
⅓ cup packed brown sugar*
¼ cup pure maple syrup
¼ cup butter, melted
1 egg
2 tsp. vanilla
1½ cups peeled and chopped Braeburn or other cooking apples
¼ cup sliced almonds

1. Preheat oven to 350°F. Coat an 8-inch square baking pan with cooking spray. In a medium bowl stir together the next four ingredients (through salt).
2. In another medium bowl combine brown sugar, maple syrup, and melted butter. Stir in egg and vanilla. Stir in flour mixture just until combined. Fold in apples. Spread batter in prepared pan. Sprinkle with almonds.
3. Bake 20 to 23 minutes or until a toothpick comes out clean. Cool in pan on a wire rack.

*Sugar Sub Choose Splenda Brown Sugar Blend. Follow package directions to use ⅓ cup equivalent.

PER SERVING *(1 piece each)* **CAL** 101, **FAT** 4 g (2 g sat. fat), **CHOL** 19 mg, **SODIUM** 96 mg, **CARB** 15 g (1 g fiber, 9 g sugars), **PRO** 2 g

PER SERVING WITH SUB Same as above, except **CAL** 94, **CARB** 13 g (6 g sugars)

Apple-Maple Snack Cake

Honey-Carrot Cake with
Mascarpone Cream

Honey-Carrot Cake with Mascarpone Cream

28 g **CARB**

SERVES 14	
HANDS ON 20 min.	
TOTAL 50 min.	

- 1¼ cups all-purpose flour
- ½ cup whole wheat pastry flour
- 1½ tsp. baking powder
- ¾ tsp. pumpkin pie spice
- ½ tsp. salt
- ¼ tsp. baking soda
- 3 eggs
- 2 cups finely shredded carrots (about 4 medium)
- ⅔ cup honey
- ¼ cup canola oil
- ¼ cup buttermilk or sour fat-free milk
- 1 recipe Mascarpone Cream

1. Preheat oven to 350°F. Grease and lightly flour a 10-inch fluted tube pan.
2. In a large bowl stir together the first six ingredients (through baking soda). In another large bowl beat eggs lightly using a fork. Stir in carrots, honey, oil, and buttermilk. Add egg mixture to flour mixture. Stir until combined. Spoon batter into prepared pan, spreading evenly.
3. Bake 30 to 35 minutes or until a toothpick comes out clean. Cool cake in pan on a wire rack 10 minutes. Invert cake onto a wire rack. Cool completely.
4. Spread Mascarpone Cream on each serving or pipe it around edge of cake on a platter.

Mascarpone Cream In a small bowl stir together **½ cup mascarpone cheese, softened,** and **1 Tbsp. honey.** Gradually stir in enough **heavy cream (1 to 2 Tbsp.)** to make piping consistency.

PER SERVING (1 slice each) **CAL** 207, **FAT** 9 g (3 g sat. fat), **CHOL** 53 mg, **SODIUM** 194 mg, **CARB** 28 g (1 g fiber, 16 g sugars), **PRO** 4 g

Zucchini-Carrot Bars

22 g **CARB**

SERVES 24	
HANDS ON 25 min.	
TOTAL 45 min.	

- 1 cup all-purpose flour
- ½ cup whole wheat flour
- 1 tsp. baking powder
- ½ tsp. ground ginger
- ¼ tsp. baking soda
- ¼ tsp. salt
- 1½ cups shredded carrots
- 1 cup shredded zucchini
- ¾ cup packed brown sugar*
- ½ cup refrigerated or frozen egg product, thawed, or 2 eggs, lightly beaten
- ½ cup golden raisins
- ½ cup chopped pecans, toasted
- ⅓ cup vegetable oil
- ¼ cup honey
- 1 tsp. vanilla
- 4 oz. reduced-fat cream cheese (neufchatel), softened
- ½ cup powdered sugar
- 1 tsp. orange zest
- 1 to 2 Tbsp. fat-free milk

1. Preheat oven to 350°F. Grease and flour a 13×9-inch baking pan.
2. In a large bowl combine the first six ingredients (through salt). In another bowl stir together the next nine ingredients (through vanilla). Add carrot mixture to flour mixture, stirring just until combined. Spread batter in the prepared pan.
3. Bake about 20 minutes or until a toothpick comes out clean. Cool in pan on a wire rack.
4. In a medium bowl beat cream cheese, powdered sugar, and orange zest with a mixer on medium until combined. Beat in enough milk to make spreading consistency; spread over uncut bars. Cut into 24 bars.

To Store Place bars in a single layer in an airtight container; cover. Store in the refrigerator up to 3 days.

*****Sugar Sub** Choose Splenda Brown Sugar Blend. Follow package directions to use ¾ cup equivalent.

PER SERVING (1 bar each) **CAL** 146, **FAT** 6 g (1 g sat. fat), **CHOL** 4 mg, **SODIUM** 92 mg, **CARB** 22 g (1 g fiber, 15 g sugars), **PRO** 2 g

PER SERVING WITH SUB Same as above, except **CAL** 135, **CARB** 18 g (11 g sugars)

Zucchini-Carrot Bars

House-Made Blonde Brownies

20 g CARB

SERVES 16
HANDS ON 20 min.
TOTAL 40 min.

Nonstick cooking spray
2 Tbsp. all-purpose flour
½ cup granulated sugar*
¼ cup packed dark brown sugar*
¼ cup canola oil
1 egg
1 tsp. vanilla
¼ tsp. salt
1 cup all-purpose flour
⅓ cup white baking pieces
½ cup roasted and salted pistachio nuts, coarsely chopped

1. Preheat oven to 350°F. Coat an 8-inch square baking pan with cooking spray. Evenly coat pan with the 2 Tbsp. flour; discard excess flour.
2. In a bowl stir together the next six ingredients (through salt). Stir in the 1 cup flour until combined. Press evenly into bottom of prepared pan. Sprinkle with white baking pieces and pistachios; press lightly to adhere.
3. Bake 18 to 20 minutes or until edges are golden brown and a toothpick comes out clean. Cool in pan on wire rack. Cut into 16 brownies.

*Sugar Sub Choose Splenda Sugar Blend for granulated sugar. Choose Splenda Brown Sugar Blend for brown sugar. Follow package directions to use ½ cup granulated sugar and ¼ cup brown sugar equivalents.

PER SERVING (1 brownie each) **CAL** 154, **FAT** 7 g (2 g sat. fat), **CHOL** 12 mg, **SODIUM** 66 mg, **CARB** 20 g (1 g fiber, 13 g sugars), **PRO** 2 g

PER SERVING WITH SUB Same as above, except **CAL** 139, **CARB** 15 g (8 g sugars)

House-Made Blonde Brownies

Butterscotch-Pretzel Bars

17 g
CARB

| **SERVES** 36 |
| **HANDS ON** 25 min. |
| **TOTAL** 2 hr. 25 min. |

Nonstick cooking spray
1½ cups powdered sugar*
1 cup creamy peanut butter
6 Tbsp. butter, melted
2 cups crushed pretzels
1 11-oz. pkg. (about 2 cups) butterscotch-flavor pieces
¼ cup heavy cream
½ cup coarsely crushed pretzels
½ cup chopped peanuts

1. Line a 13×9-inch pan with foil, extending foil over the edges of the pan. Lightly coat foil with cooking spray. For crust, in a bowl stir together powdered sugar, peanut butter, and melted butter. Stir in the 2 cups crushed pretzels. Press into the prepared pan.
2. In a medium heavy saucepan cook and stir butterscotch pieces and heavy cream over low just until butterscotch pieces are melted.
3. Spread butterscotch mixture over crust. Sprinkle with the ½ cup crushed pretzels and the peanuts; press gently. Cover and chill at least 2 hours. Using the edges of the foil, lift uncut bars out of pan. Cut into 36 bars.

To Store Layer bars between sheets of waxed paper in an airtight container; cover. Store in the refrigerator up to 1 week.

*****Sugar Sub** We do not recommend a sugar sub for this recipe.

PER SERVING *(1 bar each)* **CAL** 166, **FAT** 10 g (5 g sat. fat), **CHOL** 7 mg, **SODIUM** 154 mg, **CARB** 17 g (1 g fiber, 11 g sugars), **PRO** 3 g

Lemon Lime Bars

19 g CARB

SERVES	32
HANDS ON	30 min.
TOTAL	1 hr. 5 min.

Nonstick cooking spray
2 cups all-purpose flour
½ cup powdered sugar*
2 Tbsp. cornstarch
¼ tsp. salt
¾ cup butter
2 medium lemons
3 medium limes
4 eggs, lightly beaten
1½ cups granulated sugar*
⅓ cup half-and-half
3 Tbsp. all-purpose flour
1 drop green food coloring
   Thin strips of lemon and lime zest (optional)

1. Preheat oven to 350°F. Coat a 13×9-inch baking pan with cooking spray. Line pan with parchment paper, pressing the paper against pan and extending it over the edges of pan.
2. For crust, in a large bowl stir together the next four ingredients (through salt). Using a pastry blender, cut in butter until mixture resembles coarse crumbs (mixture will look dry). Press into the prepared baking pan. Bake 15 minutes (crust will still look dry).
3. Meanwhile, remove 1 tsp. zest and squeeze ⅓ cup juice from lemons; remove 1 tsp. zest and squeeze ⅓ cup juice from limes. For filling, in a medium bowl whisk together the next four ingredients (through 3 Tbsp. flour); divide between two bowls. Stir 1 tsp. lemon zest and lemon juice into mixture in one bowl; stir 1 tsp. lime zest, lime juice, and food coloring into

mixture in other bowl. Pour lemon filling over hot crust; bake 10 to 12 minutes or until set. Carefully pour lime filling over lemon filling; bake 10 to 12 minutes more or until set. Cool in pan on a wire rack.
4. Using the edges of the parchment paper, lift uncut bars out of pan. Cut into bars. Sprinkle with additional powdered sugar and, if desired, top with lemon and lime zest.

To Store Place bars in a single layer in an airtight container; cover. Store in the refrigerator up to 1 week.

*Sugar Sub We do not recommend sugar subs for this recipe.

PER SERVING *(1 bar each)* **CAL** 129, **FAT** 5 g (3 g sat. fat), **CHOL** 36 mg, **SODIUM** 67 mg, **CARB** 19 g (0 g fiber, 12 g sugars), **PRO** 2 g

Lemon Lime Bars

Lemon-Pistachio Slice-and-Bake Cookies

9 g CARB

SERVES 42
HANDS ON 35 min.
TOTAL 2 hr. 45 min.

- ¼ cup tub-style vegetable oil spread
- 3 Tbsp. butter, softened
- 6 Tbsp. granulated sugar*
  Dash salt
- 2 Tbsp. refrigerated or frozen egg product, thawed, or 1 egg white
- ¼ tsp. vanilla
- 1 cup + 2 Tbsp. all-purpose flour
- ½ tsp. lemon zest
- ¼ cup finely chopped lightly salted dry-roasted pistachio nuts
- 1 recipe Lemon Icing (optional)

1. In a bowl beat vegetable oil spread and butter with a mixer on medium 30 seconds. Add sugar and salt. Beat until combined, scraping bowl occasionally. Beat in egg and vanilla until combined. Beat in flour and lemon zest.

2. Divide dough into thirds. Shape each dough portion into a 4-inch-long log. Sprinkle one-third of the pistachio nuts on a sheet of waxed paper. Roll one log in the nuts to coat. Repeat with remaining nuts and logs. Wrap logs in plastic wrap. Chill about 2 hours or until firm enough to slice.

3. Preheat oven to 350°F. If necessary, reshape logs to make them round. Cut logs crosswise into ¼-inch-thick slices. Place slices 1 inch apart on ungreased cookie sheets.

4. Bake 8 to 10 minutes or just until edges are firm and tops are set. Cool on cookie sheets 1 minute. Remove; cool on wire racks. If desired, drizzle Lemon Icing over cookies. Let stand until icing is set.

Lemon Icing In a bowl stir together **1½ cups powdered sugar,* ¼ tsp. lemon zest,** and enough **fat-free milk (2 to 3 Tbsp.)** to make icing drizzling consistency.

Lemo-Pistachio Slice-and-Bake Cookies

To Freeze Place plastic-wrapped logs in a resealable plastic freezer bag and freeze up to 3 months. To prepare frozen dough, let log stand at room temperature 30 minutes to thaw. Bake as directed.

To Store Layer cookies between sheets of waxed paper in an airtight container; cover. Store at room temperature up to 3 days or freeze up to 3 months.

*Sugar Sub Choose Splenda Sugar Blend. Follow package directions for 6 Tbsp. granulated sugar equivalent. We do not recommend a sugar sub for powdered sugar in icing.

PER SERVING (1 cookie each) **CAL** 56, **FAT** 2 g (1 g sat. fat), **CHOL** 2 mg, **SODIUM** 21 mg, **CARB** 9 g (0 g fiber, 6 g sugars), **PRO** 1 g

PER SERVING WITH SUB Same as above, except **CAL** 53, **CARB** 8 g (5 g sugars)

RECIPE GUIDE

High-standards testing

This seal assures you that every recipe in *Diabetic Living® Everyday Cooking* has been tested by the Better Homes & Gardens® Diabetic Living® Test Kitchen. This means each recipe is practical, reliable, and meets our high standards of taste appeal.

Inside Our Recipes

Precise serving sizes (listed below the recipe title) help you to manage portions.

Ingredients listed as optional are not included in the per-serving nutrition analysis.

When kitchen basics such as ice, salt, black pepper, and nonstick cooking spray are not listed in the ingredients list, they are italicized in the directions.

Ingredients
- Tub-style vegetable oil spread refers to 60% to 70% vegetable oil product.
- Lean ground beef refers to 95% or leaner ground beef.

Nutrition Information

Nutrition facts per serving are noted with each recipe.

Test Kitchen tips and sugar substitutes are listed after the recipe directions.

When ingredient choices appear, we use the first one to calculate the nutrition analysis.

Key to Abbreviations

CAL = calories
sat. fat = saturated fat
CHOL = cholesterol
CARB = carbohydrate
PRO = protein

Test Kitchen tip:
Handling hot chile peppers

Chile peppers can irritate skin and eyes. Wear gloves when working with them. If your bare hands do touch the peppers, wash your hands with soap and warm water.

RECIPE INDEX

METRIC INFORMATION

The charts on this page provide a guide for converting measurements from the U.S. customary system, which is used throughout this book, to the metric system.

Product Differences

Most of the ingredients called for in the recipes in this book are available in most countries. However, some are known by different names. Here are some common American ingredients and their possible counterparts:

* All-purpose flour is enriched, bleached or unbleached white household flour. When self-rising flour is used in place of all-purpose flour in a recipe that calls for leavening, omit the leavening agent (baking soda or baking powder) and salt.
* Baking soda is bicarbonate of soda.
* Cornstarch is cornflour.
* Golden raisins are sultanas.
* Light-color corn syrup is golden syrup.
* Powdered sugar is icing sugar.
* Sugar (white) is granulated, fine granulated, or castor sugar.
* Vanilla or vanilla extract is vanilla essence.

Volume and Weight

The United States traditionally uses cup measures for liquid and solid ingredients. The chart below shows the approximate imperial and metric equivalents. If you are accustomed to weighing solid ingredients, the following approximate equivalents will be helpful.

* 1 cup butter, castor sugar, or rice = 8 ounces = $\frac{1}{2}$ pound = 250 grams
* 1 cup flour = 4 ounces = $\frac{1}{4}$ pound = 125 grams
* 1 cup icing sugar = 5 ounces = 150 grams

Canadian and U.S. volume for a cup measure is 8 fluid ounces (237 ml), but the standard metric equivalent is 250 ml.

1 British imperial cup is 10 fluid ounces.

In Australia, 1 tablespoon equals 20 ml, and there are 4 teaspoons in the Australian tablespoon.

Spoon measures are used for smaller amounts of ingredients. Although the size of the tablespoon varies slightly in different countries, for practical purposes and for recipes in this book, a straight substitution is all that's necessary. Measurements made using cups or spoons always should be level unless stated otherwise.

Common Weight Range Replacements

Imperial / U.S.	Metric
$\frac{1}{2}$ ounce	15 g
1 ounce	25 g or 30 g
4 ounces ($\frac{1}{4}$ pound)	115 g or 125 g
8 ounces ($\frac{1}{2}$ pound)	225 g or 250 g
16 ounces (1 pound)	450 g or 500 g
$1\frac{1}{4}$ pounds	625 g
$1\frac{1}{2}$ pounds	750 g
2 pounds or $2\frac{1}{4}$ pounds	1,000 g or 1 Kg

Oven Temperature Equivalents

Fahrenheit Setting	Celsius Setting*	Gas Setting
300°F	150°C	Gas Mark 2 (very low)
325°F	160°C	Gas Mark 3 (low)
350°F	180°C	Gas Mark 4 (moderate)
375°F	190°C	Gas Mark 5 (moderate)
400°F	200°C	Gas Mark 6 (hot)
425°F	220°C	Gas Mark 7 (hot)
450°F	230°C	Gas Mark 8 (very hot)
475°F	240°C	Gas Mark 9 (very hot)
500°F	260°C	Gas Mark 10 (extremely hot)
Broil	Broil	Grill

Electric and gas ovens may be calibrated using celsius. However, for an electric oven, increase celsius setting 10 to 20 degrees when cooking above 160°C. For convection or forced air ovens (gas or electric), lower the temperature setting 25°F/10°C when cooking at all heat levels.

Baking Pan Sizes

Imperial / U.S.	Metric
9×1½-inch round cake pan	22- or 23×4-cm (1.5 L)
9×1½-inch pie plate	22- or 23×4-cm (1 L)
8×8×2-inch square cake pan	20×5-cm (2 L)
9×9×2-inch square cake pan	22- or 23×4.5-cm (2.5 L)
11×7×1½-inch baking pan	28×17×4-cm (2 L)
2-quart rectangular baking pan	30×19×4.5-cm (3 L)
13×9×2-inch baking pan	34×22×4.5-cm (3.5 L)
15×10×1-inch jelly roll pan	40×25×2-cm
9×5×3-inch loaf pan	23×13×8-cm (2 L)
2-quart casserole	2 L

U.S. / Standard Metric Equivalents

$\frac{1}{8}$ teaspoon = 0.5 ml	
$\frac{1}{4}$ teaspoon = 1 ml	
$\frac{1}{2}$ teaspoon = 2 ml	
1 teaspoon = 5 ml	
1 tablespoon = 15 ml	
2 tablespoons = 25 ml	
$\frac{1}{4}$ cup = 2 fluid ounces = 50 ml	
$\frac{1}{3}$ cup = 3 fluid ounces = 75 ml	
$\frac{1}{2}$ cup = 4 fluid ounces = 125 ml	
$\frac{2}{3}$ cup = 5 fluid ounces = 150 ml	
$\frac{3}{4}$ cup = 6 fluid ounces = 175 ml	
1 cup = 8 fluid ounces = 250 ml	
2 cups = 1 pint = 500 ml	
1 quart = 1 litre	